Cook. Eat. Love.

Cucinare. Mangiare. Amore.

"...because we were not born to just pay bills and die."
A W.O.P.

To Rich,
Cook good food -
eat and enjoy what you
cook - and love all of those
who share your life. Enjoy
the book.
- Thanks again for
all your help.
Lenny Ricci
2021

Lenny Ricci

ISBN 978-0-578-79958-2

For comments, compliments, criticisms or considerations,
please email Lenny Ricci at denvrital@gmail.com.

Lenny Ricci
Aurora, CO 80247

Cover Design & Photography: Levi Pike, Redbone Media, levi@redbonemedia.net.

Names: Ricci, Lenny, author.
Title: Cook. eat. love. : a collection of Italian recipes and family stories. / by Lenny Ricci.
Description: First trade paperback original edition. | Aurora [Colorado] : Mufunzarelli Publishing, 2020. | Also published as an ebook. | Index included.
Identifiers: ISBN 978-0-578-79958-2
Subjects: LCSH: Cooking, Italian.
BISAC: COOKING / Regional & Ethnic / Italian.
Classification: LCC TX723 | DDC 641.5945–dc22

Dedication

This cookbook is for my grandmother, Irene Carfora.
She taught me that my love for cooking will not only get me hugs, praise and love; it will also bring much needed smiles to the faces of those who will grace my table for many years to come …

… and to my faithful companion and part time taste tester, Max (my cat 2003-2019), who enjoyed watching me drop things, burn things and curse a bit when things didn't go just right. He always stood by me, purring without judgement.

Thanks, Gram & Thanks, Max.

Table of Contents
– Recipes –

Table of Contents
– Stories –

FOREWORD

I guess I need to first clarify part of the title of this book.

I am Italian.

My parents were born in the United States, but their parents were Italian immigrants. In the early 1900s, those who immigrated here were rounded up on Ellis Island and put into groups. People who didn't have documentation or a birth certificate were classified as WOP's ("Without Papers"). As a kid, for as long as I can remember, we were teased by other ethnic kids calling us WOP's. My parents hated that word, but we found it intrinsic; after all, we were Italian, and all of our friends had similar "derogatory" nicknames. So, whenever I want to joke about myself in a whimsical manner, I call myself a WOP.

If you think about it, a lot of family life does revolve around cooking and eating, and in most households, loving the food that's cooked and embracing the love that is also shared at the table.

Our ancestors took many hours to prepare their meals. They were limited by what they could grow in their small private yards or what they could get at the corner market. Today, we have the luxury (if you want to call it that) of pre-packaged, processed, frozen, microwaved, and readily available ingredients that our older relatives never even imagined. With today's fast-paced world and the commonality of a two-income family, there isn't much time to devote to preparing huge homecooked meals as they did in Grandma's day. For that reason, many of the recipes I've included are easy and less time-consuming. That shouldn't stop you from getting the kids involved either. Cooking can be fun, and as I stated above, it even helps with family bonding.

If you ever spent any quality time with any older Italian man or woman, you would have probably surmised that most of them are pretty darn good cooks.

My dad was no exception. We grew up in central New Jersey where my dad owned a small pizzeria. He also served other Italian foods like pasta, chicken dishes, and lots of wonderful desserts. I like to think that I got my first taste of being a chef from working with my dad in that restaurant. I have always enjoyed cooking and creating food has always been my passion.

Dad at the Midtown Pizzeria, circa 1959

Although I was destined to become anything but a chef, it didn't stop me from pursuing cooking as a hobby. In 2007, I decided to gather up a bunch of old recipes from shoeboxes, file cabinets, sock drawers, and odd books then sat down to compile them into a cookbook. Two years later, with the addition of more recipes from family and friends and plenty of human-interest stories, I put them into book form. Unfortunately, I chose a publisher who only printed one book at a time and charged an outrageous price. That mistake kept me from becoming a best-selling author.

This new book will hopefully help me turn the tide.

So, with a sigh of relief and a glimmer of hope, I anticipate that after reading this book, you will want to call all your friends, text all of your followers on social media, and hopefully share your enthusiasm for *COOK. EAT. LOVE* with everyone!

Molte Grazie
—Lenny

INTRODUCTION

I remember vividly as a boy sitting in my grandmother's kitchen looking at all the strange things I'd never seen before. Over on one shelf there was a large two-gallon glass jar filled with little yellow round beans and water. I had no idea what they were, but I decided to try one. I reached in the jar and took out a bean to pop it in my mouth. It was salty at first and then I tasted the waxy covering and then bit into the bean itself. I spit it out. I asked my grandma what they were, and she replied, "Lupini." I think they were some kind of Italian snacks, but my family never had them. They are sold as a dry bean and are soaked in salted water for months until they become soft. Well, even soft, I wasn't thrilled with them.

The next jar I spotted was filled with what looked like long strips of yellow and red peppers with some cauliflower florets and sliced carrots mixed in. I opened the jar and took a whiff. My first thought was that these must be some kind of hot pepper treat. I decided NOT to try them. This is called giardiniera (Jar-Din-Air-Ahh).

The last two smaller jars were filled with small pea-sized green things I found out were capers, and the last jar had tiny, smelly, eel-like fish called anchovies.

After chatting with Gram, I realized that there were many new and strange things that Italians use in cooking that my immediate family was unaware of. I wouldn't begin to experiment with these until I was much older.

Most of the oddities in Grandma's kitchen were things that they were used to eating in the old country. Life was different in Sicily.

As you go through the recipes in this cookbook, it's clear that most of the ingredients called for are items that modern-day cooks have or could get access to. So, don't fret if you see something like prosciutto (Italian Ham) or parmigiana reggiano (grated cheese), as these are pretty common deli items.

I also watch from time to time some of the many cooking shows out there. When it comes to spices, many of these cooks try to measure every little thing– you know, a quarter teaspoon of this, and an eighth teaspoon of that. In my experience, with the exception of some baking, there is no reason to be so precise. Most good cooks that I have met over the years, including my aunts, cousins, and family members, just use gut feeling when adding spices. You have probably heard the phrase, "A little pinch of this and a small dash of that." I use this method all the time, which not only makes cooking fun, but most of the time the dish will turn out just fine. So, when you read, "A little pinch of this," or, "A small dash of that" in my recipes, don't overthink it. For those who insist on exact measurements, I have indulged you also.

By the way, no main Italian dish can have too much garlic.

ANDIAMO!

Have you ever had your hand smacked by a wooden spoon while trying to sneak a piece of Italian bread into a pot of Sunday sauce bubbling away on the stove? Well, I have, and it was well worth the bruise to get to sample that wonderfully aromatic garlic-and-basil infused tomato sauce. My grandma, Irene Carfora, made the best Italian sauce you have ever tasted.

Now, this is not something that can be whipped up in an hour or two. Gram's sauce takes four or five hours at least. For this reason, plan to make a huge batch and put some up in mason jars or freeze it.

I watched her making this sauce many times, and even with slight variations it always turned out great. I think I have come close to making it just the way she did. I wish there were a way to share my grandmother's broken-English accent with you while reading these recipes, but you'll just have to imagine me saying it just like she did.

GRANDMA'S SUNDAY SAUCE

- 1 lb. fresh ground beef (75-85% lean)
- 1 lb. fresh ground pork
- 2 lb. piece California roast or chuck steak
- 3-4 links mild Italian sausage
- 1/2 loaf of stale Italian bread
- Milk
- 2 large eggs
- Grated parmigiana cheese
- Salt and pepper
- 3-4 cloves fresh garlic, minced
- 8-10 large fresh basil leaves
- 1 teaspoon oregano
- 1 teaspoon thyme
- Italian seasoning
- 2 tablespoons sugar
- 1 medium onion, chopped
- 4 large cans of crushed tomatoes, in juice
- 4 large cans of tomato puree
- 1 large can of tomato paste
- 1/2 cup olive oil
- Bread crumbs, either plain or Italian style
- 4-5 large garlic cloves, thinly sliced
- **Optional:** 2 cups of red house wine such as Chianti, Burgundy, or Paisano in place of some of the added water

Let's start out with the meat. Sure, it can be made it meatless (marinara), but for now I want to share the entire recipe from start to finish. This recipe will make about eight quarts of prepared sauce.

In a medium-sized bowl, tear up pieces of the stale Italian bread and pour in enough milk to lightly soak the bread. Let this sit for a few minutes and then toss and combine the milk/bread mixture until somewhat smooth.

In a large bowl, place the two ground meats around the sides and create a well in the center. Add the eggs, about one-quarter cup of grated cheese, minced garlic, oregano, thyme, and a teaspoon of both salt and pepper. Mix the meat with the spices. Add the

bread/milk mixture and the onion and mix thoroughly. If you feel it's too "mushy," add some breadcrumbs. Take a small amount of meat and roll into a two-inch meatball. The meat should not stick to your hands, and if it does, add more bread crumbs. If you prefer, you can make the meatballs larger.

I prefer to fry the meatballs, but they can be oven baked as well. Coat the bottom of a cast iron or other heavy-duty frying pan with olive oil. Place all the meatballs in the pan close together and fry them on medium heat until they are browned on one side. Turn the meatballs and fry them on a second side. I like to turn them several times to make sure they get browned all over. Remove them from the pan and place on a paper towel to cool. Do not discard the grease from the meatballs as it will be used later in the recipe.

If you are baking the meatballs, coat a glass dish with olive oil and place them into a preheated, 350-degree oven for approximately twenty-five minutes, or until slightly browned. Remove from drippings and let them cool. Again, do not discard the grease from the meatballs as it will be used later in the recipe.

Now let's get that sauce started.

In a large stock pot (preferably one with Teflon coating), pour in about a quarter cup of olive oil. Place the garlic *slices* in the oil and heat on low temp. When you start to see the garlic bubble around the edges and turn slightly brown, turn off the heat and let them sit for about a half an hour. Remove the garlic pieces from the oil.

While the garlic is being infused in the oil, we can prepare the meat for the sauce. If you are making a marinara sauce, just eliminate this next step.

Take the chuck roast and cut it into two to three-inch pieces. Make sure to add some of the fat with the meat, most of the fat will melt with the heat and can be skimmed off later on. Cut the sausage links into two-inch long pieces.

Heat up the oil once again and add the beef and sausages. Add two to three tablespoons of Italian seasoning and brown the beef and sausages on all sides. Remove the beef chunks and sausage links from the oil. Lower the heat on the pot. I like adding additional Mediterranean oregano along with the regular Italian spices.

Add the large can of tomato paste to the pot, then fill the empty can with water and add that. Add about two tablespoons of sugar to the tomato paste and incorporate the oil with the paste. Stir this mix while heating it up (medium heat) and until it starts to bubble. Add the cans of tomatoes and fill each can three-quarters full of water and add that. For a little added flavor, you can substitute some of the added water with one of the wines mentioned optionally in the ingredients list. Stir the tomato sauce with each can of tomatoes and water added. Add about one tablespoon of salt. You can add more later if desired. Add the beef and sausages back into the pot, then add the meatballs in as well, along with all the grease. Cut up the basil leaves with a sharp knife and add to the sauce. Stir and heat on medium to low heat and cover the pot, occasionally stirring.

Now, let time take over. Check and stir the sauce every twenty minutes or so. Don't let it boil—go for a slight simmer. In about three hours, start to skim off some of the oil that will naturally form on top. I like to re-mix some of the oils back into the sauce because this is where all the flavor comes from.

Now you can see why some Italian mothers and grandmothers spend all day in the kitchen…

Here's an interesting fact. In Italy, they serve meals in courses. When you sit at a nice table in a decent restaurant, the staff will ask you to first choose your antipasto (the appetizer), then next the soup of the day, then the main course (consisting of a pasta dish), and lastly the meat. Finally, if there's any room left, the *dolce* (dessert). The Italians make dinner at least a half-day event.

In America, at least in my family, we put everything that was going to be served right on the table at the same time, including the bowl of mixed meats, salad, antipasto, bread, and the pasta. In Italy they never serve a pasta dish with meatballs. That's an American thing, but I personally love my spaghetti *with* meatballs.

If the plan is to jar the sauce, make sure the sauce is boiling and that the glass jars have been sitting in boiling water for at least twenty minutes. Begin to fill, leaving about a half-inch below the rim. Place a full basil leaf on the top and seal immediately with a rim and cap. Place the jars upside down on a soft towel in a cool place. When cooled, test each jar to make sure the center of the lids "pop" down and are sealed properly before storing permanently. They will stay good for a year or so if they are sealed properly. Feel free to freeze the meatballs, beef, and sausage separately in zip bags or include them right in the jars of sauce.

When freezing the sauce, first let it cool completely before filling, using "freezer style" plastic zip bags. Leave about an inch of space for expansion. Lay the bags flat in the freezer, and never use a microwave to defrost the sauce while it's still in its plastic bag. Instead, place the frozen bag in cold water and let it defrost naturally.

Okay, if you just spent all that time making the meatballs and Sunday Sauce and you have a few extra bucks left, I would suggest making braciole (bra-zhole) and adding it to your sauce. This isn't typically found at many restaurants because it's time consuming and expensive, so not too many will attempt it. Once you do, though, you will never again skip making braciole.

BRACIOLE

1 lb. fresh round steak
1/2 cup Italian seasoned breadcrumbs
1 bunch fresh parsley
3-4 garlic cloves, chopped
Salt and pepper
1/2 large onion, cut into small chunks
1/4 cup parmesan cheese

If buying meat from a butcher, have the shop slice the round steaks very thin—about a quarter inch. Arrange the meat slices on waxed paper or plastic wrap then tenderize the meat with a cleaver or mallet. Cut the meat into approximately three by seven-inch pieces. Place a generous amount of chopped parsley on the meat, leaving some space around the edges. Sprinkle with parmesan cheese and then press the garlic into the meat along with the cheese and parsley. Add some onion and sprinkle with a little salt and pepper. Now add the bread crumbs and pat everything down. Starting with the longer side, roll up each piece of braciole and secure with at least three pieces of string at the ends and in the middle. The tighter the better for searing. Place a cast iron frying pan (or other Teflon-coated pan) on the stove and preheat without any oil. Once the pan is hot enough, roll the pieces of meat on the hot skillet with a spatula or large wooden spoon, pressing slightly until they are browned. Add a bit of olive oil and cook them for only a few minutes, if that long, then place them into the pot of simmering sauce. The braciole need to cook for almost as long as the sauce so they become nice and tender and juicy. A word of caution: these meats will fall apart easily if cooked too long, so remove them from the pot if you sense that they are getting over cooked. Cut the strings and serve alongside the other meats and the pasta.

PASTICOTTI

Everyone wants to impress family and friends with their culinary skills and this next dessert recipe is going to make you the talk of the family. At first you might say, "I can't do that," but I'm going to say, "Yes you can."

This wonderfully decadent dessert is called pasticotti (pronounced Pasta-Chaut-ah). It hails from the Salento or Puglia region of "The Boot" in Italy.

These vanilla custard-filled sweet pastries are great for a dinner party, or even breakfast with a nice cup of espresso or hot chocolate. They can be frozen for a week or so, but it's better to use them up within a few days of making them. Let's get started.

For the Pastry:

2 cups all-purpose flour

2/3 cup sugar

1 egg, room temp

1-1/2 teaspoon good vanilla extract (not flavoring)

Pinch of salt

1/4 cup soft butter

1/4 cup regular or butter flavored Crisco

1/4 cup whole milk

For the Custard:

3 heaping tablespoons corn starch

1/2 cup sugar

1/2 cup heavy or whipping cream

1 cup whole milk

3 small or medium egg yolks, slightly beaten

2 tablespoons soft butter

1-1/2 teaspoon almond extract (not flavoring)

Optional: 1 egg, beaten (for egg wash)

Fill the cups, making a dome for the crust.

The baked pastries can be frozen for a week or two.

A medium cupcake tin will work, but I prefer small 3-inch fluted tart pans that I purchased from Bed Bath and Beyond for about 85 cents each.

With a decent food processor, making this dough is a breeze. The recipe is a longer process without one, but it will turn out just fine.

Follow the same directions if using a bowl instead of the food processor.

Mix the flour and sugar together and pulse a few times. Add all the other ingredients and pulse after each addition. Keep the machine running until the dough forms a ball and doesn't stick to the sides of the bowl. Split the dough into two pieces and wrap each in plastic wrap. Refrigerate the dough.

Making the custard is pretty straightforward, just note that a metal whisk is best, and use medium heat—don't try to rush it.

Mix the cornstarch and sugar together in a medium-sized pot, preferably with Teflon coating.

Add the milk and whipping cream, and heat just until tiny bubbles appear on the edges of the pot. Add the beaten egg yolks and whisk them into the milk mixture. Continue whisking the mixture until it gets thick, usually about six to eight minutes. Remove from heat and add the almond extract and softened butter. Press a piece of plastic wrap onto the surface of the custard. This will prevent a skin from forming on the top while it cools. Once cooled, refrigerate the custard.

Now comes the fun part of assembling the pastries. Roll out one section of dough on a floured surface to about 1/8 inch thick. For a heartier crust, make them thicker, but note that the recipe will yield fewer pastries. By the way, this recipe makes about a dozen three-inch cakes.

Cut out three-inch rounds of dough using a drinking glass or a cookie cutter. Spray the tart pans or cupcake pans lightly with cooking spray or use Crisco shortening.

Place a three-inch dough round into the bottom of the pans. If using fluted tart pans, conform the dough into the fluted sides and push the dough up close to the top, leaving just a little pan showing below the top rim. Continue to prepare the rest of the pans with the dough rounds.

Roll out the rest of the dough and cut out additional three-inch rounds.

Fill each of the tarts with about two heaping tablespoons full of custard, smoothing it out along the top edge of the pans. Place the top piece of dough on the custard and pinch the dough down on top of the bottom crust to seal them.

An important note: refrigerate the pastries for at least two hours before baking.

Heat the oven to 325 degrees. Using the additional beaten egg, brush the egg mixture on top of the pastries, sealing all the dough with egg wash.

Place in the center rack of the preheated oven and bake for approximately fifteen to twenty minutes or until golden brown on top. Remove and let them cool in the pan. Once cooled, remove them from the pans and let them cool completely on a dish towel or wooden cutting board. Sprinkle the pastries with powdered sugar before serving. These go great with some vanilla or chocolate gelato on the side.

If you are like me, you really enjoy sharing food with friends and family. I recently visited my sister and some of my extended family living in New Jersey. Even while on vacation, I didn't mind doing some cooking and giving my sister a break from the kitchen.

I decided to make something simple, but special—something they probably would never make themselves: spaghetti with puttanesca sauce.

When I first discovered this dish, I experimented with many spices to finally come up with my own blend that I think works best.

Puttanesca in Italian means "mean spirited lady" but here is the official scoop. In some towns in Italy in the 1940s, there were plenty of "loose women" lurking around. Since the war was just ending, there were also a number of "anxious" men. Some ladies of the evening had to get creative in order to secure the wanton affections of these men, so they resorted to cooking this dish. Puttanesca sauce, when cooked just right, gives off the most powerful of aromas. Once they lured the guys in and fed them, well, it's easy to guess the rest of *that* story.

I make up small batches of the spices for this sauce and package them in small plastic zip bags, void of all air to keep them fresh. One packet is enough for one pound of pasta, so if I am cooking two pounds, I simply double the recipe and use two packets of spices.

PUTTANESCA SAUCE

For one pound of pasta:

1 tablespoon Mediterranean oregano, finely ground
1 tablespoon marjoram
1 tablespoon dried basil leaves
1 teaspoon ground black pepper
1 teaspoon crushed red pepper flakes (use less if you like it less spicy)
Pinch of sugar
2 tablespoons chopped fresh or dried parsley
1 teaspoon salt

Combine all the above spices and place them in a small zip bag. Take as much air as possible out of the package and seal it.

If making dinner right now, don't bother with the above step.

Once the spices are set aside, it's time to prepare the sauce.

2 large cans of crushed tomatoes or 4 small cans (peeled whole tomatoes will also work, but they will need to be crushed by hand over the pot)

1/4 cup grated cheese

1 large Vidalia onion, chopped

1 cup sliced black olives (for a saltier flavor, use pitted Kalamata olives, sliced)

1/3 cup virgin olive oil

5-6 large garlic cloves, sliced thin

Optional: 4-6 anchovy fillets (finely chopped)

1/4 cup capers

3-4 fresh basil leaves, cut in strips for garnish

1 lb. cooked pasta (linguini, thin spaghetti, penne, or angel hair), *al dente* (this means just a bit undercooked and chewy). Watch out for the angel hair; it cooks really fast.

Drain the pasta but preserve some of the hot water to thin the puttanesca sauce if needed.

Do not rinse the pasta; pasta sauces tend to cling onto pasta better when not rinsed.

Add the olive oil to a large, deep sauté pan. Heat on medium for a few minutes and then add the onion and the garlic slices. Continue to heat until the garlic is just lightly browned, and the onion is soft. Add the tomatoes and heat for a couple of minutes. Add the entire bag of spices and the olives. Heat until bubbling. Cooking time varies, but letting it simmer for at least twenty minutes or until it thickens is best. Lastly, add the capers and anchovy fillets if using them. If the sauce is too thick, use some of the reserved pasta water to thin it. Remember, the thicker it is, the better it will adhere to the pasta.

Add the pasta directly into the pot to warm up and serve immediately, or single serve the sauce in dishes with the pasta on bottom. Sprinkle with grated cheese and chopped fresh basil leaves for a great looking dish. And if you are a wine drinker, I suggest a slightly chilled Chianti or Montepulciano Abruzzo. Your taste buds will thank you.

I found a piazza named for my family while traveling in Rome.

I was born in Jersey City, New Jersey. My parents were born here, but their parents were immigrants from Italy. My dad served in the merchant marines and after getting married, settled in Jersey City. Countless immigrants came over from the motherland and settled in sections of north and central New Jersey, creating defined areas that each became known as "Little Italy." Tradesmen would open small retail shops – delis, bakeries, and gift shops—and entire families would work in the stores. I remember hearing stories about growing up poor with lots of kids, cousins, nieces, and nephews all living in large tenement housing on the same block.

Since almost everyone was in the same socio-economic class, people were friendlier, kinder, and more generous to each other. People went out of their way to greet everyone, and everyone on the street knew everyone else and all their families. Weekends on the streets of Jersey City were like block parties, with everyone sitting on stoops, kids playing in the streets, and even pizza vendors hawking fresh pizzas in a metal box strung around their necks.

As poor as we were, we always ate well. Some recipes came over with the grandparents and were handed down through the family to share. Pasta e Fagioli is a peasant dish my grandmother shared with her daughter and eventually with my dad. We had a small brood growing up and this meal, as cheap as it was, never failed to fill us up. Some people call it pasta fazool or pasta with beans. It can be made in a variety of ways, with any type of beans from pork and beans, cannellini, great northern white, or chickpeas. I have made this so many times, and with each variation it tastes just a little bit different. For a poor man's meal, though, it is simply the best.

PASTA E FAGIOLI

8 oz. good quality bacon, diced

1 medium onion, chopped

3-4 medium garlic cloves, sliced thin

1/8 cup good quality olive oil

3 cups or 2 15-oz. cans of beans (great northern, cannellini, white or red kidney, chickpeas, garbanzo, or pork and beans). Feel free to mix any of these together, depending on what's on hand. *Do not discard the liquids.*

2 large cans of crushed tomatoes

Pinch of crushed red pepper flakes

1/2 teaspoon dried oregano flakes

1/2 teaspoon mixed Italian seasoning or substitute a pinch of thyme, rosemary, basil, and sage

Salt and pepper to taste

Grated cheese

1 cup red table wine like Chianti, Burgundy or Merlot

1 lb. macaroni (just as with the beans, any pasta or macaroni product will do, from ditalini, small shells, elbow macaroni, or mini penne).

In a large and deep cast iron frying pan, add a small amount of olive oil, the sliced garlic, and chopped onions. Under medium heat, lightly brown the garlic and then add the bacon. Cook until the onion and bacon are well cooked but not crisp. Open the cans of beans and pour in the beans, including the liquid. Again, mix and match any of the types mentioned. Add the wine.

Add the cans of tomatoes to the pan and mix. Taste the sauce for flavor and add salt and pepper as needed. Stir the sauce a few times, every five minutes or so for about twenty minutes total, then add the crushed red pepper flakes. Cover the sauce. If the mixture is too thick, add some hot water, but it's best to leave it quite thick to mix with the pasta. Continue cooking on medium or low heat for approximately forty minutes.

Cook the pasta as directed but do not rinse it. I like it a bit chewy, so I always cook it al dente—just slightly undercooked. Once cooked, dish the pasta into bowls and add the sauce. Serve with grated cheese on top along with some red wine and garlic bread. Warning: this is a very filling meal, so don't overdo it. Have a cannoli for dessert with some nice sweet red wine.

I was always very excited to hear when my grandmother was coming for a visit. That meant that she would take over the kitchen and I would get to help her prepare some delicious foods. One particular Sunday when I was maybe 12 or 13 was no exception. Gram showed up with her fifty-year-old suitcase in hand. After settling in the spare bedroom, she would don her flowered apron and walk out into the kitchen. After discussing things with Mom, dinner plans would be made. I, of course, was never too far away when she visited.

I loved hearing her tell old time stories of growing up in a quaint Sicilian neighborhood in Italy. She would talk about the village butcher shop and mom-and-pop grocery store. Gram would tell me about the town bakery where all the ladies would bring loaves of their homemade bread to bake in the giant ovens. I could just imagine the aromatic smell of fresh baked Italian bread wafting through the town square.

I would get around to asking what she was going to make for supper and this day she said, "How 'bout we make some fresh pasta?" Well, I nearly fell off my chair in anticipation. I didn't know that was even possible!

"Let's make some cavatelli," she said. They are pretty easy and lots of fun to make. I'm going to share that with you now. By the way, we call them *gavadeel.*

CAVATELLI

2 cups fine semolina flour
1 cup all-purpose unbleached flour
Salt
A couple tablespoons good olive oil
1 cup warm water
Grated cheese

Stir together the semolina and flour in a bowl along with about one teaspoon of salt. Add two tablespoons of olive oil. Add enough warm water to form a stiff dough. Turn the dough onto a floured workspace and knead the dough for about three minutes. The dough should be smooth and elastic. Add more flour as necessary so it doesn't stick to your hands or the work area. Shape the dough into a ball and cover it with plastic wrap. Let the dough rest for about a half hour.

Now, if you want to really get into the spirit of making homemade pasta, skip the bowl and use the kitchen or dining room table. Pour the flours and salt into a small circle, then add the olive oil and water to the center. With your fingers, grab a small amount of flour and incorporate it into the water/oil mix. Continue mixing in the rest of the flour while kneading it into a ball. Once all combined, cover with plastic wrap and let it rest.

Pull off a chunk of dough about the size of a tennis ball and using your hands, roll it out on a floured surface. You want to create a rope about a half-inch thick. With a sharp knife, cut the rope into half-inch pieces. Using your middle and pointing finger together, push a dent into the center of each piece of dough. At the same time, pull the piece toward you. It will curl up. You want it to have a tube shape but not be connected together.

Spread some flour on a large white towel, or other cloth, and place the cavatelli on them to dry. If you are not going to use all of the pasta, place them on a floured tray and put them in the freezer. Once firm, transfer to a plastic bag and remove as much air from the bag as possible. They will stay good in the freezer for months.

Continue cutting and rolling the rest of the dough and letting the cavatelli dry on the table. Place them into slightly salted boiling water and cook for about five minutes. They will float to the top after a while. Test them for doneness. You want them to be just slightly chewy.

Top the macaroni with some of your delicious Sunday Sauce, adding grated cheese to the top.

My friend and personal trainer, Greg, and I were talking about food, which we often do while working out. We started discussing the usual—healthy foods; but then the conversation drifted to rather simple meals that don't take much time to prepare but nonetheless impress.

I mentioned steak pizzaiola. Greg had never heard of it, so I thought I would enlighten him.

I like to use fresh plum tomatoes for this dish, only because they are easy to prepare and have incredible flavor. There is a little prep involved, but all in all you can have dinner ready in twenty to thirty minutes. Let's get cooking.

Kitchen Tip: When buying fresh tomatoes for preparing any Italian dish, always let them sit out on the counter for a few days until they are just slightly over ripe and soft to the touch. This way you can guarantee you are getting the most flavor from those mouth watering fruits and your food will taste the freshest.

STEAK PIZZAIOLA

4 small 8-oz. sirloin steaks, cut thin

6 large ripe plum tomatoes, chopped with all juices

4-6 large garlic cloves, minced except for 4 to 6 thicker slices, separated

Salt and pepper

Fresh basil

2 teaspoons Mediterranean oregano

12-15 medium to large pitted black olives, sliced

Pinch of crushed red pepper

Small amount of flour on a large plate

Trim some of the fat off the steaks and gently pound them with a meat tenderizer.

In a small pot add about 1/8 cup olive oil. Add the minced garlic and heat on medium heat until the garlic is slightly brown. Add the chopped tomatoes, the oregano, and about a half teaspoon of salt. Let the tomatoes cook for seven to eight minutes. Add the crushed red pepper and 1/4 teaspoon of regular black pepper.

Prepare a frying pan with 1/8 cup olive oil and drop the sliced garlic into the oil. Heat on medium. Drop the tenderized steaks into the plate of flour one at a time. Coat both sides with flour and then flip them and coat the other side. Continue with the other pieces of meat.

Place the coated steaks into the frying pan and cook for five minutes on each side or until slightly brown. Pour the tomato mixture directly on top of the steaks and simmer for another five or so minutes. If you are using an inexpensive cut of meat cover and simmer on low for at least thirty minutes for a nice tender steak. Add the black olives. If there is extra sauce, serve the steaks with a small amount of penne pasta on the side, cooked al dente. Don't forget the garlic bread, grated cheese, and a slightly chilled glass of merlot. Serves 4.

Did I mention that I come from a very large Italian family? I was smack dab in the middle of the nine, and I am the oldest of the boys. Mom wasn't much of a cook. One would think that having a husband who owned a pizzeria and restaurant that she'd be somewhat adept at cooking. Well, that wasn't the case in our house. My older sisters did most of the cooking, and when I was tall enough to reach the knobs on the gas stove, I was also indoctrinated into the ways of the kitchen. Not being much of a sports guy, I found it more rewarding to make food rather than touchdowns.

Between what I learned from my grandmother, my dad and my sisters, I managed to create some tasty meals. Speaking of tasty, I must share a little funny.

My second oldest sister, Rene, met and married a guy named Mike Fornicola. At some point we were invited to his mom's house for Sunday dinner. Nana was right off the boat and spoke very little and mostly broken English. I'm not even sure what Nana made but my youngest sister went up to her and said, "Nana, that was really good. What did you put in it to make it so tasty?" Nana looked straight at my sister and said in her broken English, "What a tasty? I no putta no tasty in there." We all just sat there and cracked up.

One of my favorite "Tasty" breakfast or lunch dishes is one that my mom used to love. I liked to call it "Mary's Frittata" and I named it after her. For this meal, you can sneak in any extra veggies you have on hand. There is no set rule about what can or cannot be added.

Kitchen Tip: Don't rinse your spaghetti or other pastas when they are finished cooking. Simply drain them and let them sit until ready for use; stirring occasionally. Your sauce toppings will stick to the pasta and you won't have that watery mess on the bottom of the bowl.

MARY'S FRITTATA

6-8 large eggs

Milk

5-6 medium sliced green or yellow zucchini, peeled and sliced about 1/4 inch thick

2 heaping tablespoons grated parmigiana cheese

2 small onions, sliced thin

6 oz. grated mozzarella, Monterey jack, Swiss, or any combination of these cheeses

3-4 roma tomatoes, sliced

2 garlic cloves, sliced thin

Optional ingredients: sliced mushrooms, sliced red or green pepper strips, mild Italian sausage links (cooked and sliced), 1 medium potato, sliced thin

I like using a heavy-duty cast iron skillet for this because it cooks nice and evenly. You can also use a Teflon coated deep frying pan.

If planning to use mushrooms, peppers, and/or potato, cook those ingredients first. Add some olive oil to the pan and heat on medium. Sauté the garlic with the potatoes and mushrooms and peppers until they are just starting to wilt, about three to four minutes. Add the sausage slices and cook an additional two minutes. Remove from pan and set aside.

If sticking just with zucchini, add some olive oil and the garlic to the pan, then cook on medium for about three to four minutes. Add the zucchini and turn each piece over to coat them in the oil. Add the onion.

Cover the pan and cook for about ten minutes or until the zucchini slices become slightly browned. You will need to turn them quite a bit, over and over.

Mix the eggs, some milk, grated cheeses, parmigiana cheese, and a bit of salt and pepper in a bowl. Whisk for a few minutes until fluffy. Pour the egg mixture onto the zucchini. Turn the heat to low and cover the pan. Once the edges start to bubble up, shake the pan to prevent sticking. If the center isn't quite cooked, place the cast iron pan under the broiler in the oven for a few minutes. If you are adventurous, try flipping the entire omelet onto the lid and then sliding it back into the pan to brown the top. I have lost a few omelets this way, so make sure you are comfortable doing it. Serve with the sliced roma tomatoes and a garnish of sliced basil or parsley. This frittata will serve about six hungry people.

If you are preparing this dish with mushrooms, peppers, sausage, and potatoes, add them just after the zucchini are slightly browned and before adding the eggs. Finish the recipe as written above.

If you were anything like me growing up, you probably watched one of the most endearing, yet most frightful, movies ever created: *The Wizard of Oz*. I, like hundreds of thousands of kids, always hated the Wicked Witch of the West. With every viewing around Thanksgiving time, we all rooted for the kind ones, the meek and timid, and the underdog. The lady that played the part of the Wicked Witch, Margaret Hamilton, was typecast as a villain, a monster, and this persona never did change in the minds of us kids.

One day I was at a garage sale in our neighborhood and came across a small spiral bound cookbook simply called *Cora's Country Cookbook*. The photo on the front was of Margaret Hamilton, all dressed up in a blue and white flowered top with a darker blue fancy apron holding a lattice topped cherry pie. Seeing on the cover a photo of the woman who terrified us, caused nightmares, and was just the pinnacle of evil piqued my interest. You just don't think of the person playing a role as a perfectly decent person living a normal life just like you. As I thumbed through the first few pages, I remember something she wrote. "Nothing good is ever easy. Balderdash!! Everything is easy—once you know how to do it."

I plunked down my 25 cents and took the book home. As I read through it, with almost every recipe there was a short quote, simply, "Cora says," then it was on to the recipe. There was no mention of her as an actress, no mention of *The Wizard of Oz*, no mention of her being typecast as a villainous woman. Just this woman named Cora who published a country cookbook for all to enjoy. I also remember her doing commercials for Maxwell House coffee. Remember "Good to the last drop"?

I cherished that little cookbook and from time to time I refer to it if I am making something old fashioned, like biscuits and gravy or stick-to-your ribs Savory Beef Pot Roast. I want to share one recipe from Cora's cookbook with you that I have made so many times. It's easy and takes less than a half hour from start to finish.

CRANBERRY MUFFINS

Cora says: "Tart cranberries add wake-up flavor to these family-pleasing muffins."

1-3/4 cups all-purpose flour
2 tablespoons sugar
2-1/2 teaspoon baking powder
3/4 teaspoon salt
1 large egg, beaten
3/4 cup milk
1/3 cup vegetable oil
1 cup chopped raw cranberries
3 tablespoons sugar

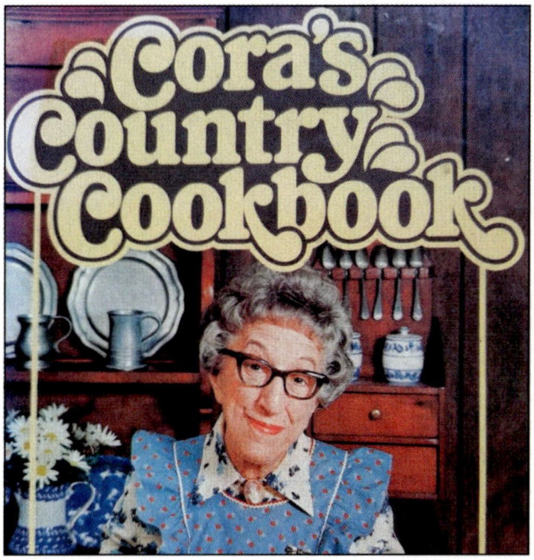

Mix the flour with the two tablespoons of sugar, then add the baking powder and salt.

Combine the milk with the beaten egg and add it to the flour mix. Add the oil and blend until just dampened. Sprinkle the cut-up cranberries with the three tablespoons of sugar and lightly stir them into the batter. Spoon the batter into ten greased muffin tins filling about 2/3 full. Bake at 400 degrees for about twenty-five minutes or until a toothpick inserted in the middle comes out clean. Cool and serve. Makes 10 muffins.

Growing up in the fifties was tough. With a lot of mouths to feed, my dad had to work extra hard to earn enough to keep us all fed and clothed. He worked for the New Jersey Turnpike Authority driving a Caterpillar, owned and operated a gun shop, flung pizzas in a restaurant window, and even worked as a mechanic at a gas station or two. Dad was always a stickler for having dinner on time. He insisted that dinner be on the table at 6 pm and everyone be present around the dinner table. Most weeknights, it was usually pasta or chili or something that could be whipped up in as little time as possible.

One night I remember dad coming in from work, washing up, and coming into the dining room to eat. Almost everyone was seated but something was missing: the food.

Dad looked at his watch, looked at us kids, then looked at his watch again. Then he started yelling. “Can’t I come home just one time and find my dinner waiting for me?” Then, “Why is it so much trouble to get my meal when I sit down?” He continued, “I work hard all day. Is it too much to ask to have supper ready at 6 o’clock?” With each statement, his voice got louder, and with each comment, his face got redder. When my sister Celia finally brought out the bowl of spaghetti and set it on the table, dad had finally reached his limit. Noticing that the food was cold, he picked up the large bowl and flung it at the wall. There was spaghetti hanging from the dining room fixture, and there was tomato sauce oozing down from the ceiling. There were glass shards sticking out of the wall board and there were seven kids sitting there all about to cry. Dad charged out of the room and left all of us in a state of disbelief. Needless to say, there was no dinner that night. I seem to recall that no matter how hard we worked at cleaning up that mess, the walls always seemed to have a nice orange tint for many years after. Here is another pretty easy and quick meal to make if you have seven kids and a hard-working man waiting patiently for their supper.

RIGATONI CON BROCCOLI

1/2 cup (more or less) extra virgin olive oil
2-3 pats of butter
5-6 large garlic cloves, sliced thin
2-3 cups broccoli florets (no stems), preferably bite-sized pieces
1 cup low-sodium chicken broth
1 lb. rigatoni or ziti, cooked al dente and drained
10-15 medium-to-large fresh basil leaves
Bunch of fresh parsley, chopped, no stems
Grated parmigiana or pecorino Romano cheese
Salt and pepper to taste
Optional: crushed red pepper flakes

Pour the oil and butter into a small but deep stock pot. Using medium heat, fry the garlic until slightly brown. Remove the garlic. Increase the heat a bit and throw in the broccoli florets. Toss the florets until they turn dark green (this should take just a few minutes). Try to work quickly as the broccoli will become mushy and lose its deep color if cooked too long. Add the chicken broth and put the garlic back into the pot. Add some salt and pepper to taste. Tear up five to six basil leaves into small pieces and add them along with some parsley. Add the cooked pasta and toss. Consider adding more olive oil if it seems too dry. Finally, add the pepper flakes, again according to your taste (crushed red pepper flakes are potent).

Cut the remaining basil leaves into thin slices and dish the pasta into a bowl. Garnish with grated cheese, the basil, and more parsley if you want. Serve right away as this dish cools quickly. Some good garlic bread and a glass of slightly chilled Cabernet Sauvignon will go nicely with this dinner. Serves 6.

One of my all-time favorite movies is called *Fatso*. It stars Dom DeLuise and Anne Bancroft. From the title, you can guess that it clearly involves an overweight Italian and food. Anne Bancroft wrote and directed the movie and DeLuise played the main character, "Dominick DiNapoli." The movie was both funny and sad at the same time, showing the best of Italian cuisine and how one could easily overdo eating and become obese. DeLuise was fantastic in this 1980 film.

In 1988, DeLuise wrote a cookbook called *Eat This... It'll Make You Feel Better*. In the book he details many of his magical childhood memories of his growing up in an Italian neighborhood in Bensonhurst, Brooklyn. The title of his book also made me reflect on my own memories of growing up in a large Italian family. Although we kids were very active—always outdoors, always playing in the fresh air and sunshine, we never got fat or even sick for that matter.

What I do remember is when we did get a scraped knee or a bruised elbow, we always ran inside to get bandaged up and were always rewarded with a cookie or piece of cake or something sweet. I guess all mothers think that if you eat that kind of thing, it'll make you "feel better." It must be an Italian thing. As a tribute to the late Dom Deluise, I would like to add one of his own recipes from that cookbook. It's also one of my favorites as well.

CHICKEN OR VEAL PICCATA

- 1 lb. veal scaloppini or chicken breast, thinly cut
- 1 cup flour with 2 teaspoons black pepper and 1 teaspoon salt mixed in
- 4 tablespoons butter and 1/8 cup olive oil
- 1/2 or 1 lb. fresh mushrooms, cleaned and sliced
- 1 large lemon
- 1 cup half-and-half or table cream
- 2-3 tablespoons dried parsley
- 1/2-3/4 cup dry white wine such as chardonnay or sauvignon blanc
- Fresh parsley
- Extra lemon slices

Cut the veal into small serving pieces and coat each one in flour on both sides. If using chicken, slice each one in half, place a piece of plastic wrap over the pieces on a wooden board, and tenderize with a mallet. Coat each piece on both sides with the flour mixture. In a skillet, heat the butter and olive oil on medium until it sizzles. Add the meat and cook over medium heat until lightly browned on both sides. If using veal, cook only a few minutes—these cook really quickly. Once all the pieces are browned, remove the meat from the pan. Add the sliced mushrooms and the wine and sauté until lightly browned. Roll the lemon along the counter while pushing down to loosen the juices. Cut the lemon and squeeze the lemon juice into the pan. Mix the juices gently and cook for an additional minute or two. Add the half-and-half and use a whisk to stir while it thickens. Add the chicken or veal back into the pan and cover with sauce. Warm the meat. Serve with extra lemon slices and fresh parsley sprigs. Serves 4.

I like serving linguine with garlic and oil with this dish and some additional dry white wine.

Let's face it, we Italians know good food. Our foods are rich in calories and flavor. Most everyday people who want something Italian won't put in the time and effort to cook Italian food the way I would. Why do you think the Olive Garden is the number one Italian fast food chain in the world? But even dinner at the Olive Garden is too time consuming for many people, so they buy pizza frozen or from a ton of chain places.

As I mentioned earlier, most of the recipes in this cookbook will be quite easy to prepare, and I hope to lure you and your family away from the fast food places and back into a cozy dining room where the group can sit down with some great food and fewer large screen televisions.

My friends describe the Olive Garden's version of Chicken Francese as being the best thing on the menu. It's a simple chicken dish prepared with lemon and wine. Even the worst cook in the world won't ruin whatever it is that's on the menu if he or she is cooking with wine and lemon. Let's try my version.

CHICKEN FRANCESE

1 lb. chicken breast fillets, thinly sliced
2 eggs, beaten
3/4 cup all-purpose flour
3/4 cup chicken broth
1/2 cup white wine
3 oz. lemon juice
1/4 cup olive oil
1/4 cup melted butter
Parsley
Salt and pepper

Tenderize the chicken breasts to about a quarter-inch thickness. Dredge them in the flour with some salt and pepper added.

Dip the floured cutlets in the beaten egg and once again back into the flour. Set them aside.

Mix the broth, wine, and lemon juice together in a measuring cup.

Heat the oil and butter in a deep-frying pan until it sizzles. Add the chicken pieces but don't crowd them. Cook on medium heat for about three minutes on each side or until golden brown. Remove from the pan and finish cooking the rest of the cutlets. You might have to add a bit more oil and butter to the pan depending on the size of the fillets. Place the cutlets in a warm place.

Add the chicken broth/wine mixture to the pan and swish around the browned pieces and juices. Cook until thickened. Add a palmful of parsley. If there isn't enough gravy, add more wine, lemon juice, and chicken broth, then a bit of flour, to make more. Once you have enough, place the cutlets back into the pan and heat them up, being vigilant to not overcook them. Serve immediately with any extra gravy, lemon slices, and more parsley on top. I like serving a green vegetable along with some mashed potatoes on the side, but some thin spaghetti with the gravy works too. One pound of sliced chicken breasts will serve four people.

Kitchen Tip: Always allow grated cheese to reach room temperature before serving. It will be more fragrant and enhance the flavor of food.

Having a large family not only puts a strain on the monthly budget, but after the expenses, there was little money left for frugal things kids like such as ice cream, candy, and cookies. If it wasn't something we could make, we usually went without.

Among dad's income makers was a small gun shop he ran in Port Reading, New Jersey. It wasn't a large shop, but some of his clients weren't exactly on the up and up, if you know what I mean.

Good fortune came our way when dad was making a deal with one of his gun store buddies who also happened to work for the Quaker Oats Company. He might have been an exec of some sort. One of his handgun sales took place between this man and my dad right on the floor of

the factory in Elizabeth, New Jersey. As dad was making the exchange of money for the gun, he noticed huge bags of cookies sitting on the floor near some machines. Dad questioned the man about the bags, and he said that they were all the broken cookies that came off the assembly line during the day shift. He told my dad that they couldn't sell them and donated them to charity. Dad told the guy, that, well his family ***was*** charity, so the guy said to take 'em. Dad dragged home this huge fifty-pound plastic bag of broken cookies.

You should have seen our little faces light up staring at that large bag of sweet goodies. Even though it was mid-July, the bag contained lots of freshly baked Christmas cookie pieces among many others. We weren't ashamed at all to eat broken cookies.

Speaking of cookies, and keeping with the theme of easy recipes, here is one I know you'll enjoy.

ORANGE JUICE COOKIES

1/3 cup granulated sugar

1-1/2 sticks unsalted butter, at room temperature

3 large eggs, at room temperature

1 teaspoon vanilla extract

1/2 cup orange juice, with pulp, at room temperature

3 cups all-purpose flour

2-1/2 teaspoons baking powder

ICING

2 cups confectioners' sugar

1/2 cup orange juice, with pulp

1/2 teaspoon vanilla

In a deep bowl, mix the softened butter, eggs, vanilla, orange juice, and the sugar then mix with a mixer until well combined. Add the flour and baking powder then mix with a spoon until mixed. You may have to add more flour to keep the batter from sticking to the fingers.

Take a large spoonful of batter and roll into a ball. Place each onto an ungreased cookie sheet about two inches apart. Press the tops with the bottom of a small glass dipped in flour to about a quarter-inch thick.

Bake in a 350-degree oven for about thirteen to fifteen minutes or until lightly browned. Let them cool ten minutes before removing them to a wire rack to cool completely. This recipe will make about 36 medium sized cookies.

Mix the ingredients for the icing and use the back end of a spoon to spread a nice thick coat on each cooled cookie, then let dry. For a nice touch, grate a little bit of navel or mandarin orange zest on top before the icing sets.

You can also change this recipe into **LEMON JUICE COOKIES** by substituting lemon juice for orange juice and using freshly grated lemon zest in the recipe as well as grated on top of the finished cookie.

I have many memories of my dad, some good and some not so good. As my brothers and I grew up there was lots of "fixin'" to do. Let's face it, kids tend to break plenty of stuff. Dad was meticulous about his hand tools and his work bench. He had every tool one can think of, from five different kinds of pliers to four different hand saws. Most of the smaller tools like screwdrivers were mounted on a huge peg board, and each and every tool was outlined in black marker. If for some strange reason Dad happened to see an empty spot on that board, all hell would break loose. Not only was he meticulous, but also quite anal about anyone using a tool without him knowing about it. One day while digging in the back yard, he came across an old rusted pair of gas pliers. Within a few minutes all three of us boys were lined up next to his workbench and like a witch trial, we were grilled, ridiculed, and sentenced to severe punishment. Of course, no one owned up to taking the tool. After our reprimanding, I noticed that there were no empty pegs on the peg board. I quietly and meekly told dad of my discovery and well, there was no apology. Some Italian dads are pretty stubborn and not likely to admit any sort of wrongdoing.

What he did do next was rather unexpected. He asked what our favorite dinner in the whole wide world was, and the three of us immediately shouted out in unison, "Lasagna!"

That night he made the biggest tray of lasagna he could, and we were once again three happy little boys. As it turned out, the found tool belonged to the father of one of the neighborhood boys and it just happened to get buried in *our* back yard.

DAD'S LASAGNA

1 lb. lasagna noodles, al dente
2 quarts of **SUNDAY SAUCE (page 16)** or marinara sauce
1 3-lb. container of whole milk ricotta
1 lb. whole milk mozzarella, grated
2/3 cup parmigiana cheese, divided into 3 parts
Salt and pepper
Fresh parsley
3 eggs
Pinch of nutmeg
Sliced mild or hot cooked sausage, in 1/4-inch slices, or cooked meatballs, cut into small chunks
Fresh basil leaves for garnish

I have tried making my lasagna using the "no boil" lasagna noodles, but for me, well, they just don't seem to come out the way I like. This recipe will use the tried-and-true "boil 'em first" type of noodles.

Slightly under-cook the lasagna noodles in a large pot of water with a little salt added. Drain them and lay them over the edge of a large colander to dry. Heat the oven to 350 degrees.

In a large 10"x13" glass or metal pan, pour some sauce on the bottom of the pan and cover it entirely.

Start by laying one layer of lasagna noodles lengthwise, overlapping the ribbed edge by about a half-inch. Cut smaller pieces to line the short edge.

Mix the ricotta with the eggs, a good handful of fresh chopped parsley, a handful of grated parmigiana cheese, and a pinch of salt and pepper. Add the nutmeg. Don't overmix the ricotta.

Divide the ricotta into two equal parts and layer the first layer of noodles with the first part of the ricotta. Spread half of the mozzarella cheese on top of the ricotta. Layer some sauce on this and if adding meat, space meatballs or sausage over that layer.

Start the second layer of noodles and repeat the above steps. There should be enough ingredients for this second layer. Use up the remaining ricotta and mozzarella cheeses.

On the top, add the last layer of noodles, pour on a good amount of the sauce, sprinkle with the remaining parmigiana cheese, and tightly cover the pan with foil. Place the baking dish on a large cookie sheet in case it boils over and bake in the preheated oven for about thirty minutes. Remove the foil and check to see if the center is bubbling; if not, continue baking until it is. Once the center is bubbling, let cook for an additional ten minutes or until the ricotta is set.

Some members of my family also like their lasagna to have a nice crunchy top layer. If you want yours like that, set the oven to broil and keep the lasagna in the oven for five or six more minutes. Watch it carefully so that it doesn't burn. Remove and let cool for about ten minutes before cutting. Pour some extra sauce on top, sprinkle on a little parmigiana cheese, garnish with basil leaves, and serve with garlic bread and a decent glass of slightly chilled chianti.

You can also make this a veggie lasagna. It's pretty similar except that the recipe incorporates some raw vegetables. I use broccoli, red and green peppers, yellow and green squash, cauliflower, and sliced mushrooms. For more color, add some thinly sliced or grated carrots. Slice the zucchini and squash thinly and cut the broccoli florets and cauliflower into small, bite-sized pieces. Thinly slice the peppers then cut the strips in half.

Layer some sauce on the bottom of the pan, then place a layer of noodles to cover the sauce. Add the ricotta cheese, layer whatever veggies you want, spread some grated mozzarella cheese, and add a little grated parmigiana cheese. Then repeat with a second layer. The top layer will be just noodles, a generous amount of sauce, and some grated parmigiana cheese. Cover tightly with foil and bake at 375 degrees for about forty-five minutes. Check after thirty minutes, remove the foil, and continue baking until the center is bubbling. Add more time if necessary. Let cool about fifteen minutes before cutting into squares. Serve with some extra sauce on top, a sprinkle of parmigiana cheese, and maybe a basil leaf or two. Don't forget the chianti: my favorite red is Montepulciano d' Abruzzo. Try it—you'll love it. This recipe will make about 12 4"x4" squares.

Did your parents ever threaten you when you wouldn't eat your broccoli, if you pulled your sister's hair, or if you accidentally flushed your brother's GI Joe doll down the toilet? I'm sure they did. Did they ever threaten you with going to your room without supper? I'm sure they did. You must have done something pretty awful for them to say, "If you don't stop that, I'm going to sell you to the Gypsies." Parents will try anything to make their little darlings behave, like the infamous, "Just wait until your father gets home, then you'll see."

The first time you hear that, you really stop behaving like a spoiled imp and sit quietly with your hands folded on your lap. The second time they use that technique, you catch on, and when the punishment by dad never materializes, you know you got away with murder.

Mom and dad's engagement photo

There was one memorable evening when we all sat down to dinner and mom served a very unpopular dish called tripe. For those who don't know what tripe is, well, to be kind, it's cows' stomach. When scraping the bottom of the barrel, you must resort to meals that will fill a kid's belly. Tripe is cut into small, bite-sized pieces and boiled in a red spaghetti sauce, seasoned with some hot pepper flakes and parsley. I'm sure this is a delicacy somewhere, but for the Ricci kids, it was like death in a bowl. There were lots of snickers and grins, and some of us with a more outgoing personality just got up and left the table. Tripe is like eating bubblegum without the sugary syrup. You can chew and chew and chew some more and you never quite get the stuff squashed enough to swallow. Needless to say, Mom would threaten us with all of the above-mentioned threats and even the, "Wait until your father gets home" bit. For those particular dinner nights, all the kids were happy to go to their rooms without supper.

Another not so popular meal was liver and onions. Now, I must say that I really love liver. This was a hit or miss at our dinner table. Some of the kids really liked it, while some had the same distaste for this as they did for tripe. Some just couldn't get past the smell of it cooking. There aren't too many dishes one can make with liver, so when I do make it, it's just liver and onions with a potato side dish.

I am including this recipe just because it is so uncommon to find it in any cookbook.

CALVES' LIVER

1-2 lbs. baby calves' liver
Flour
Salt and pepper
3-4 large Vidalia onions (sliced thin)
1/4 lb. good quality bacon
Olive oil for frying
1/2-3/4 cups chicken stock or broth

Len and sis, Nora, around 1951

Slice the calves' liver into quarter-inch thick slices. Heat about six slices of bacon in a heavy-duty Teflon or cast-iron pan. Don't overcook the bacon but get enough fat extracted to fry the meat (or add some olive oil if needed). Add the sliced onions. Cook for eight to ten minutes, or until the onion becomes wilted. Dredge the slices of liver in flour with some salt and pepper added. Dab the flour on the meat with your fingers and let the pieces dry for a few minutes on the dish. Transfer the onions and bacon to another dish. Heat the oil again and add more if needed. Place the liver slices in the oil and cook for only a few minutes on each side. Once you flip them, add the onions and bacon back into the pan. After cooking all the liver, cover with foil and move the meat and onion mix to the oven on low heat until ready to serve. Add some chicken broth to the oil/bacon mix in the pan and heat until a nice, thick gravy results. Scrape all the bits from the bottom of the pan and when it is thick enough, transfer to a gravy boat. If the gravy is too thin, add a tablespoon of flour or corn starch to one-eighth cup of chicken broth. Stir and pour slowly into the hot frying pan while whisking. This will produce a thicker gravy.

Serve the liver with the onions and bacon and pour on some gravy. A side dish of scalloped potatoes goes really well with this meal, along with some fresh sliced Italian bread and some red wine – like a good pinot noir. This recipe will serve 4-6 people depending on the portion size of liver.

If you have never had to deal with the frustration of an automated phone call, you probably are living on a different planet than mine. I happened to be having an issue with my Internet being down and called my local provider for service: *"THANK YOU FOR CALLING CENTURY LINK. YOUR CALL IS VERY IMPORTANT TO US. PLEASE STAY ON THE LINE AND THE NEXT AVAILABLE AGENT WILL BE WITH YOU IN A MOMENT." (wait…wait…wait…)*

"Hello."

So, I'm all set to tell the agent about my issue when I hear, *"WE'RE SORRY FOR THE DELAY. PLEASE REMAIN ON THE LINE FOR THE NEXT AVAILABLE ASSISTANT." (bizzzzz…bizzzzz…bizzzzz)*

Then I hear, *"THE NEXT AVAILABLE AGENT WILL BE WITH YOU IN APPROXIMATELY THREE TO EIGHTEEN MINUTES." (bizzzzz… bizzzzzz…bizzzzz)*

Great, I think to myself, putting the phone on speaker and leaving it on the counter. Then comes that horrible "on hold" music that was once performed on the Johnny Carson Show while three clowns were spinning plates on their noses.

Then, suddenly a break in the music and I think to myself, *Oh good—only four minutes*. Now I get to talk to a real live person. But NOOOOOOO! *"THANK YOU FOR HOLDING. WE ARE TRYING HARD TO GET TO YOUR CALL."* By then, I curse under my breath and slam the phone back down. This goes on for another twenty-two minutes while I start to prepare dinner. I found a package of mild sausage links which were nearing expiration, so I took them out to defrost while pondering the creation of a really delicious meal I call rigatoni with sweet sausage and tomato sauce.

I got so caught up in the smell of the sausage cooking that I completely forgot all about that stupid clown music playing, the Internet being down, and my pissed off mood with the wireless company. I grabbed the phone, said a couple of very nice Italian words I can't repeat here, pushed the end call button, and went back to my cooking. I love how making delicious food always puts me in a good mood and calms me down. Enjoy the recipe.

Kitchen Tip: If you're not sure the baking powder in your cupboard is still good, try this: fill a glass half full of hot water. Put in a half teaspoon of baking powder. It should bubble like crazy if it's still good to use. If not, discard it. For baking soda, put a little in a glass jar and add some vinegar. It should fizzle right away if it is still usable.

Italian Street Fair, Astoria Queens, NY—Smell that Sausage!

RIGATONI WITH SWEET SAUSAGE AND TOMATO SAUCE

1 lb. mild or hot Italian sausage

2 large cans of chopped peeled tomatoes with juice, or 2-3 lbs. plum tomatoes, peeled, seeded, and chopped

2 large garlic cloves, minced

1/2 cup dry white wine

1 lb. rigatoni pasta, cooked al dente

Pinch of oregano, dry basil, and black pepper

2-3 tablespoons olive oil

4-5 fresh basil leaves, torn into pieces

1/2 cup fresh grated cheese

Optional: crushed red pepper flakes

Cook the pasta al dente and set aside. Do not rinse the pasta.

Remove the sausage from their casings and finely chop the meat. In a large Dutch oven, pour in the olive oil, then add the sausage meat and the garlic. Heat on medium heat while stirring the sausage meat. When the meat is slightly browned, add the wine and bring to a simmer. Cook on low heat until the wine evaporates.

Stir in the tomatoes with the juices, add the basil, a bit of salt, and a pinch of pepper. Cook on low heat until the sauce thickens, about forty-five minutes, or longer if necessary. Add the cooked pasta to the tomato sauce and heat thoroughly. Serve with grated cheese on top. Serves 6. Chocolate Mousse is a nice light dessert to serve with this dish.

One summer day in July way back when, I had this really crazy idea of getting my unusually large family and some of our friends together to take a bus trip to Hershey Park in Pennsylvania. After calling some bus companies, making lots of arrangements with everyone in the family, and getting all the details worked out, we set out at 6 am aboard a

chartered bus from Academy Bus Company. Everyone met at a parking lot in the local middle school and we set off. Once everyone was on board, I took my trusty clip board and started down the aisle counting heads and collecting money. There were about fifty of us, family, friends, and friends of friends. We sang songs, played car games, and sipped coffee and biscotti. In the back of the bus were five or six large ice chests full of sandwiches, snacks, fruit, and drinks. Once out of New Jersey, we took Interstate 80 West through the beautiful hills of eastern Pennsylvania. The trip took about three hours, but it went by quickly, with only a few minor bits of bickering among the kids.

We got to the park around opening time and spent the entire day going on thrill rides, water rides, and sickening rides, plus taking in some great shows. Since everyone was scattered all over the park, we arranged to gather for lunch at the picnic ground at 1 pm. After lunch it was back to the fun. Around 6 pm, we got back on the bus with a lot of very tired and spent children and adults. Our driver had spent the day in town and, well, let's just say he might have had a few. As we headed out of Hershey back onto the interstate, some of us noticed that he was a bit too heavy on the gas and making a few too many scary turns. To top it off, we ran right into a serious thunderstorm. With many heads thrashing from side to side, my brother Pat decided to have a chat with the good driver. Luckily, he slowed down and stopped the erratic driving. We did make it home safely that night and avoided ending up on the front page of the Sunday papers.

While we're on the subject of chocolate, let me share one of the best chocolate cake recipes you will ever find. This cake is so rich you'll think you went to chocolate heaven on a cloud and back.

Kitchen Tip: A sure fire way to make your chocolate cakes, brownies, cookies and cupcakes taste extra chocolaty, add a teaspoon of instant coffee to the recipe. The coffee crystals won't give it a coffee taste, but rather a deep mocha flavor.

EXTREME CHOCOLATE CAKE

1-1/2 cups all-purpose flour

3/4 cup Hershey's Special Dark Unsweetened Cocoa

2 cups sugar

1-1/2 teaspoon baking soda

1-1/2 teaspoon baking powder

1 teaspoon salt

2 large eggs

1 cup whole milk

1/2 cup vegetable oil

2 teaspoons pure vanilla extract

1/4 cup espresso coffee

3/4 cup boiling water

Heat the oven to 350 degrees. Prepare two 9-inch cake pans by cutting two parchment paper circles just shy of nine inches. Brush the bottom lightly with shortening, and place the parchment paper down. After smoothing out the parchment paper, brush the bottom and sides with more shortening.

Mix all the dry ingredients in a large bowl. Add the eggs, milk, oil, vanilla, and coffee, then beat with a mixer on medium speed for four minutes. Slowly pour in the boiling water and mix well. The batter will be thin. Divide into the two prepared pans. Place the pans on the center rack of oven and bake for about twenty-five minutes. Test with a toothpick in the center until it comes out dry. Do not overbake. Remove from oven and let cakes cool. I like this cake with a chocolate ganache, which is just a pourable chocolate icing. I'll add the recipe for the ganache.

For the filling, try this delicious chocolate mousse. It's like a fluffy chocolate pudding.

CHOCOLATE MOUSSE

1 envelope of unflavored gelatin
1/4 cup cold water
1/3 cup boiling water
1 cup sugar
2 teaspoons corn starch
2/3 cup Belgian, Swiss, or Special Dark Hershey Cocoa
2 cups (1 pint) heavy cream or whipping cream
2 teaspoons vanilla extract
1/8 cup any flavor liqueur (Gran Marnier, Chambord, or amaretto)

You will need two deep bowls, one larger than the other. Pour the cold water in the smaller bowl and sprinkle the gelatin over it. Let set for about five minutes. Add the boiling water and stir until clear and smooth. Set this aside.

In the larger bowl combine the cocoa, sugar, and corn starch then mix it well. Add the whipping cream and vanilla. Beat with a mixer until it is very thick. Slowly add the gelatin mixture and liqueur, then mix until combined. Pour into dessert dishes and cool completely. If you are using for a cake filling, let it cool completely before assembling the cake layers.

CHOCOLATE GANACHE

One 8-oz. Hershey Special Dark chocolate bar
1/4 cup heavy cream or whipping cream
1 tablespoon soft butter
1-1/2 teaspoon creme de cacao, light or dark liqueur

Combine all the ingredients except for the liqueur and heat over low heat until smooth and silky. Stir in the crème de cacao and cool until lukewarm. Quickly pour over cake and if necessary, spread with a knife or spatula. Usually this is enough for just the top of the cake, with a little spilling over on the sides.

For as long as I could remember, I have always been a tinkerer. My two younger brothers were into sports and outdoor stuff, while I on the other hand enjoyed reading books—especially electronic related books. I was, as one might say, the olden-day equivalent of Sheldon Cooper of *The Big Bang Theory* fame. I always had a fascination with how things worked and what made things tick. My intrigue of mechanics led me to explore the inner workings of many items I found around the house. I always wished that stuff would break down, just so I could take it apart and find out why. I dissected flashlights, clocks, mom's mixer, and even my sister's Chatty-Cathy Doll. When she got that doll for Christmas one year, and showed it off, I knew right there and then that I would have to somehow get a hold of it and take it apart to see what made it talk. Unfortunately, Cathy would never survive the brutal dismantling that took place three weeks later. I not only got a good scolding, but I had to give my sister my allowance for fifteen weeks so she could buy a new one. I learned a valuable lesson: I was welcome to take apart anything of mine, but everything else was strictly taboo.

I finally ran out of things to take apart and became interested in chemistry. I started doing odd jobs in the neighborhood to make enough money to buy some glassware and chemicals, and my dad let me turn one corner of the basement into a makeshift laboratory. I spent many hours after school mixing and creating until one night when I accidentally mixed up some Sulphur with some hydrochloric acid, and, well, it wasn't a pretty sight. The smell of rotten eggs wafted up into my parent's bedroom and next thing I knew my entire lab was being carted away to the garbage dump somewhere in Piscataway, New Jersey.

I really enjoyed chemistry. I realized that all things are made up of combinations of different chemicals and even the slightest changes to those could make a totally different outcome.

Even at a young age, I learned that food is also made up of chemicals and that adding and mixing certain things totally changes the way something tastes. Like my old chemistry lab in the basement of the house, I now have amassed a large collection of spices in my kitchen with which I love experimenting. Some obscure spices like lavender or coriander can completely change the flavor and taste of a simple homemade biscuit or beer bread.

One of my favorite obscure spices is anise extract. This flavoring smells like black licorice and is quite strong. Some folks add just a drop or two in a small cup of espresso coffee or cappuccino.

I use it for flavoring one of my favorite snack cookies: pizzelle. These thin, crunchy, almond and licorice flavored cookies go great with the aforementioned cappuccino or espresso and even on a cold winter night with some hot chocolate. A pizzelle maker is required to make them. They are available on Amazon or at Bed, Bath and Beyond for about $40." Here is my recipe for pizzelle.

PIZZELLE

1-3/4 cups all-purpose flour
2 teaspoons baking powder
3 large eggs, at room temperature
3/4 cup pulverized almonds (use a food processor)
3/4 cup granulated sugar
1/2 cup unsalted butter, melted
1 teaspoon anise extract

In a small bowl, mix the flour and baking powder. In a second bowl combine the eggs and sugar. Using a mixer on medium speed, mix for a minute or two until it is thick and creamy. Add the melted butter and the anise extract. Alternately add the flour and the almonds until just combined. Try not to over mix the batter.

Heat the pizzelle maker and drop about two teaspoons of dough in the middle of the patterned surface. Close the lid and bake until lightly browned. This varies with the heat setting, but once you've done a couple, you get the right amount of dough and the right amount of cooking time. Remember, the lighter brown, the better.

Use these cookies to create ice cream cones. Just roll them around a cone-shaped dowel or by hand. You can also make cannoli shells by using metal cannoli sleeves. Just make sure to roll them immediately from the pizzelle maker, while they are still hot. Makes about thirty 6" cookies.

Serve them warm with powdered sugar and watch them disappear.

I was born in July 1948, the first boy for my parents. I had four older sisters at the time. As more and more kids came, they knew we needed more room. Dad purchased an old gray fifteen-room house on Third Avenue in a little-known sleepy town of Port Reading in central New Jersey. The house was huge, and it had plenty of bedrooms to accommodate our large brood. We no longer had to sleep like crewmen on a submarine. The house had steam heat, a large back yard, and a beautiful wrap-around front porch. Dad was a whiz at fixing just about anything that was broken—a window, door frame, you name it. So, this old house kept him pretty busy with repairs.

Although my dad had many talents and jobs, he enjoyed cooking more than anything. This prompted him to go to work at a local bar/pizzeria in the next town over. The owner let my dad run the kitchen and when business started to dry up, dad convinced him to do something drastic.

Dad got together with some of my uncles, George, Frank, Tino, and Phil, and a few of their Saturday evening poker buddies, Sal, Johnny, and Tony. Together they decided to break down the front of the bar and put in a giant picture window, move the pizza oven and workstation to the front of the store, and pipe the exhaust from the giant oven right out into the street. It was the smartest thing they ever did. My dad attracted the attention of two local journalists and when the grand opening was revealed, dad's photo was splattered all over the front page of the evening newspaper. "Ricci's Pies Fly—to Entertain the Crowds." And crowds there were. People stopping by on the sidewalk were truly amazed watching my dad flip that dough in the air and catch it on his fist. He would twirl it around again and again and set it down on a pie tin smoother than a plane landing. I can still see that wide grin on dad's face in that picture; he had an air of confidence that equaled a guy on a flying trapeze. Of course, this *was* the entertainment because many of these people had never seen anyone flip pizza dough before.

I remember dad telling me that "you always have to outsmart the competition," and "Don't be afraid of change, because it will always work itself out in the end." However, certain things just don't need changing. My dad's recipe for Escarole soup was handed down from his mom, who brought it over from the old country. This soup's origins include a version that includes tiny meatballs and it was called Italian Wedding Soup. In some old villages in Italy, a wedding was a community event. The parents of the bride usually held a street festival and anyone and everyone was welcome. Since most of the people were poor, they had to stretch their budget and make *abbondanza* (abundant dishes) to feed the multitudes, and this soup did the trick. Large pots of steaming broth with locally grown romaine lettuce, white beans, and meatballs were dished out in bowls and served on long wooden tables. Folks would help themselves to wine, garlic bread, and soup then mingle with the town's folk. Some of these Italian weddings would last from morning to midnight.

The recipe that follows will make enough soup for about fifteen people, but since you are going through all this trouble, you might just want to freeze or jar some of it for later enjoyment or perhaps for someone's wedding.

ITALIAN WEDDING SOUP

2-3 large heads escarole (romaine lettuce), washed, rinsed, and cut into small pieces

1-2 lbs. chicken (breast or thighs), cut into bite-sized pieces

2-3 dozen tiny meatballs (recipe to follow)

1 extra large onion, chopped into small pieces

3/4 cup sliced or chopped celery with lots of top green leaves also chopped

3/4 cup sliced carrots

1-1/2 cups orzo pasta, thin egg noodles, or pastina, al dente

6-8 cups low-sodium chicken broth

Optional: 2-3 hardboiled eggs, chopped

In a large stock pot, add the escarole pieces. Add the chicken broth and carrots and cook for about thirty minutes or until the leaves are wilted and the carrots tender. Set aside.

In another smaller pot, place the chicken, onion, and celery with leaves. Cover with water and bring to a boil. Reduce heat and simmer until the chicken is tender, about twenty minutes. Pour this into the larger stock pot with the greens. Add more broth if necessary. Keep on low simmer while preparing the meatballs.

1-1/2 lbs. ground beef
3/4 lb. ground pork
2 medium eggs
1/2 cup onion, minced
1 cup plain breadcrumbs
1/2 cup grated parmigiana Reggiano or pecorino cheese
Salt and pepper to taste
Handful of cut fresh parsley

Mix all ingredients and roll into one-inch balls. Drop right into the simmering greens and broth. Cook for about an hour until the meatballs are tender. Add the chopped eggs if desired and the cooked pasta. Serve with the grated cheese. Depending on the size of the serving bowl, this should feed about 8 hungry people.

Now that you have tried the escarole soup, you will want to make the variation with beans called Manesta. Some tried and true Italians will just call this "Shcarole." This one is a bit heartier and great for dinner on a cold and damp winter's eve.

MANESTA & BEANS

2 cans white cannellini beans (also called great northern beans)
1/8 cup olive oil
3-4 garlic cloves, minced
6 strips good quality bacon, cut into small pieces
4 medium-sized heads of escarole, washed, rinsed, and cut into small, bite-sized pieces
8-10 fresh basil leaves
1/2 teaspoon ground oregano (I prefer Mediterranean oregano)
Plain breadcrumbs
2 large cans of low-sodium chicken broth

You will need one large stock pot and a deep-frying pan.

Pour the chicken broth in the large stock pot. Add the escarole. Next add enough water just to cover the greens. Gently boil (covered) until they are tender, for about an hour. Set aside and do not drain.

In the frying pan, add the oil, garlic, and bacon. Heat on low and sauté the bacon and garlic until slightly brown. Try not to overcook the garlic. Add the two cans of beans including the juices. Cut the basil into small slices and add this to the pot. Add the oregano, and to spice it up a little, add some crushed red pepper flakes. Add salt and regular black pepper to taste. Stir and lower the heat. Cover and cook for about forty minutes, stirring occasionally.

Drain the escarole and save some of the liquid. Mix the beans and greens together and heat again. If there is too much liquid, add some breadcrumbs to thicken it. It should be somewhat soupy, but thick like clam chowder. If it is already too thick, add some of the broth from the escarole to thin it. Serve with grated parmigiana cheese and garlic bread.

If I live to be 100, I will never forget Miss Kay Miozi. None of the kids remembers exactly where she fit into the lineup of either family or friend, but nevertheless, she was an interesting part of my childhood. Kay was around 40 years old, about five feet eight inches tall, and fairly skinny. She wore flannel shirts and jeans almost every time I saw her, and she acted more like my uncle than my aunt. She smoked Tiparillo cigars, drove a beat-up old Chevy pick-up truck, and could do any kind of a chore a man would do.

My dad did lots of odd jobs to make money and one was to pick up large mail sacks from the local post office and deliver them to the train station in a town a few miles away. Back in 1959, they still ran coal fired locomotives on the track which ran the main line from New York to Southern New Jersey. These engines were huge, spewed tons of smoke, and were really loud.

Since I was a big train buff from day one, I never missed an opportunity to visit the train station. Dad usually made the mail run about three times a week, but one time he was tied up with something else and asked Kay if she would do it. I was within earshot of this request and begged to tag along. Kay agreed, and off we went. When we got to the Middletown train station, Kay dragged the mail bag out of the back of the pickup and hoisted herself up on the platform and placed the bag on the large spike hanging off the mail pole. The bag would be snagged by a trainman as the train went whizzing by. Kay told me to stay put in the cab of the truck so as not to be in the way. She also told me not to touch anything! Well, being the curious little guy that I was, I couldn't resist turning all the dials and pushing any button that looked interesting on the dashboard. Well, I made the mistake of pushing in the cigarette lighter and not realizing that it had gotten stuck. It started the dashboard on fire. I panicked and looked around for something to put out the fire. All I saw was a five-pound bag of raw lentils lying on the seat. I grabbed the bag and ripped it open with my teeth and threw the lentils at the flames and at the smoke pouring from the dash. That helped a bit, but Kay saw the smoke and the commotion. She came running over, tore off her jacket, and put out the fire. The dashboard was ruined, and I was severely punished for that little mishap. I also had to drag out Mom's Electrolux vacuum and clean up every single one of the strewn lentils. Even worse, there were no lentils left to make one of my favorite meals—Lentil Soup with Italian Sausages.

LENTIL SOUP WITH SAUSAGES

8 oz. mild Italian sausage meat (or links without casing)

6 medium garlic cloves

1/4 cup olive oil

1 medium onion, chopped

2 large cans of low-sodium chicken broth

1 cup dried lentils

1 large can (28oz.) of Italian stewed tomatoes with basil

2 tablespoons Worcestershire sauce

1/2 teaspoon oregano

1/2 teaspoon black pepper

1/4 teaspoon ground cumin

2 medium carrots, sliced thin

2 celery stalks, sliced thin

2 cups fresh spinach leaves, torn into pieces

Optional: 1 bay leaf

Soak the lentils overnight in cool water. In a large saucepan, heat the oil and sauté the onion and garlic together until lightly browned. Add the ground sausage and chop into small, bite- sized pieces while browning. Add the chicken broth. Rinse the lentils and add to soup. Squeeze the tomatoes into small pieces and add juice and all to the soup. Add all the spices and bring to a boil. Lower the heat and let it simmer slightly, uncovered, for about thirty minutes. Bring soup to a boil once again and add the carrots, celery, and spinach. Lower the heat and simmer for one-and-a-half to two hours. If the soup gets too thick, add more water to thin it. Remove and discard the bay leaf if you added it. A good Chianti, some Italian bread, and parmesan cheese will top off this meal. Serves 6.

Most kids I knew had at least two favorite holidays. Halloween was second. In our house, it was a big deal. We always rushed home from school with anticipation of trick-or-treating and getting lots of candy, money and the eventual stomach ache that night.

My Aunt Kay lived in Jersey City and would always drive down to the Jersey Shore with her kids because they didn't live in a kid-friendly neighborhood like we did. In Hazlet, there were rows and rows of houses all close to one another, so a kid could cover lots of ground in no time at all. We could count on getting at least a half a pillowcase full of goodies in under two hours. Our attic was stacked full of chests with old clothes in them and it didn't take much time to dig through them and come up with some interesting get-ups. We always helped our cousins with costumes conjured up from the vast collection of creepy clothes we found up there. My aunt always insisted on feeding us homemade chicken soup before we went out trick-or-treating. As like most New Jersey nights in October, this particular Halloween night was a very cold and damp one. I loved the taste of Aunt Kay's chicken soup, so hot and delicious with lots of chicken pieces and tons of grated cheese on top. Her soup always helped keep us goblins nice and toasty warm while we went scavenging the neighborhood.

THE RICCI's
(Back): Maryann, Judy, Irene, Lenora
(Front): Celia, Richard, Kathleen, Len, Pat

AUNT KAY'S HOMEMADE CHICKEN SOUP

1 whole chicken, cut up
1 small bunch of celery (with leaves—very important), sliced on an angle
1 lb. carrots, sliced on an angle
1 large yellow onion, sliced thin
3-4 teaspoon poultry seasoning (I prefer Bell's Poultry Seasoning)
1 lb. orzo pasta
8 quarts water
1 teaspoon black pepper
4 teaspoon salt
3-4 bouillon cubes, if needed
Grated pecorino Romano cheese

Boil the chicken for at least ninety minutes on a low, rolling boil. *Important*: Keep the pot covered.

Remove the chicken from the pot and let it cool so you can handle it.

Tear off all the chicken from the bones, cut it into small, bite-sized pieces, and drop them into the broth. I like adding some chicken skin also as it melts and gives a really good flavor to the broth. I discard the gizzards, heart, and liver, but add them if you wish.

Add all the vegetables to the broth and return to a boil. After fifteen minutes, add the poultry seasoning and salt and pepper. Take a taste before adding much salt. If there isn't enough chicken flavor, add some bouillon cubes, but remember, these contain added salt too. Cook the orzo pasta separately and add to the bowls before adding the soup. Garnish with grated cheese. This pot of soup should serve 12 kids or 8 adults easily.

In keeping with the soup theme, I must re-tell a story from my childhood that to this day I still find amusing. The story revolves around a little old lady who was a relative of someone's great aunt or sister's husband's niece or someone like that. We never really knew. Her name was just Zi Marie!

"See! I told you she was still there!" I said to my little brother Richie as we stared innocently at Zi Marie. There she sat in the corner of the kitchen at my aunt's house on a plush red chair pushed right up against the table. Zi Marie was very old and she drooled. She didn't just drool a little. Her tongue was always hanging out of her mouth and she drooled onto the paisley flowered apron she always wore. She stared at us, blank as a sheet of white paper, and we stared right back trying to figure out if she was still alive. Zi Marie was always there when we visited– always in the same spot in the kitchen, always wearing the same paisley apron. We think they kept her around for the sole purpose of using her tongue to moisten the S & H green stamps we got from grocery stores to redeem for great gifts. In all seriousness, Zi Marie was a pretty good cook in her day. She made a "to die for" (no pun intended) Stracciatelle Minestrone Soup. I managed to get the recipe from my mother who got it from my aunt who learned it directly from Zi Marie.

ZI MARIE'S STRACCIATELLE MINESTRONE SOUP

This recipe is in two parts, soup and meatballs, and will serve eight to ten people.

Soup:

1 quart low-sodium chicken broth
2 cups water
1/2 cup pastina macaroni or 1 cup bow ties
1/8 teaspoon thyme

1 teaspoon parsley

2-3 medium carrots, sliced thin 1/2 lb. fresh spinach leaves

1 16-oz. can of garbanzo beans (chickpeas)

2 15-oz. cans of Italian stewed tomatoes with herbs

2 eggs, beaten

Grated parmigiana cheese

In a large stock pot, combine all the ingredients except for the beaten eggs and bring to a boil. Turn the heat to low and simmer while preparing the meatballs.

Mini Meatballs:

1 lb. ground beef, 85 percent lean

1 egg

1/4 cup Italian seasoned breadcrumbs

2-3 tablespoons grated cheese

Handful parsley flakes or chopped fresh parsley

1 small onion, chopped

3-4 garlic cloves, minced

Mix all the ingredients in a small bowl and make one-and-a-half-inch round meatballs and put them into the simmering soup. Turn the heat up to medium and cook for about an hour. Once the meatballs are tender, turn the heat to high and bring to a boil. While stirring the soup, slowly pour in the beaten eggs. Immediately remove from the heat and let it sit for a couple of minutes. It's now ready to serve but don't forget the grated parmigiana cheese.

Consider these variations:

Add thin slices of pepperoni to the soup instead of meatballs.

Add small slices of semi-cooked hot or mild Italian sausage instead of meatballs.

Oh, and remember to have some hard-crusty Italian bread on hand to sop up this incredible broth. Eat this hearty soup, but whatever you do, try not to drool.

We had a neighbor who lived next door to us on Mason Drive in Hazlet, New Jersey. Jean was divorced from her husband, Warren, and was raising her three young children on her own. She was an R.N. and her shifts at the local hospital were mixed and varied. Sometimes the kids were home alone, and my mom would look after them for a few bucks. Sometimes Mom would run into the ex-husband who would stop by unannounced to see his kids. Warren was a loner who worked the late shift at a local manufacturing company. Back in the day, we never locked our doors or cars, and stealing or robbery was uncommon in our neighborhood.

One night around 1:00 am we were awakened by noises of pots and pans clanging in our kitchen. Mom got up first followed by two of my older sisters and me. As we sleepily wandered into the kitchen, we came upon Warren. "What the heck are you doing here at this hour of the morning?" Mom asked.

"I was lonely and needed to chat with someone over coffee," he replied.

"Well, it's awfully late!"

"I know," he said, "but Jean said you were always up late."

Mom was always too nice to anyone in need, so she dragged out the coffee pot and brewed a pot of coffee. That night she stayed up and comforted Warren until 3:00 am when he finally left. After a few times a week of this, Mom told good ol' Warren that she couldn't keep this pace up as she had to get up for work herself in the morning. That didn't stop Warren from coming over whenever he felt like it, getting out the coffee pot and making himself at home in our kitchen. We often heard him come in, make a pot of coffee, and sit there all alone until he finished it and left. We dubbed him "Warren Coffee," our official midnight visitor. After a few more visits, the kids would leave subtle hints for Warren like, "Here's a jar for tips," and, "Crumb cake goes really good with COFFEE!"

I decided to leave a nice handwritten note asking him to occasionally bring over some chocolate eclairs and leave one with my name on it. I guess he got the hint and started bringing over goodies which always got eaten the following morning or taken to school for snacks. Warren always brought over the best eclairs, made with fresh creamy custard filling and semi-sweet chocolate icing on top. Over the years, I've had many a good éclair, but none ever came close to those I finally made myself. So, in honor of Warren Coffee, here is my recipe:

ECLAIRS

For the Custard Filling:

3 egg yolks, beaten

2 tablespoons cornstarch mixed with 2 tablespoons all-purpose flour

1-1/2 cups whole milk

1/2 cup sugar

1 teaspoon pure vanilla extract—pinch of salt

In a small saucepan, combine the sugar, salt and cornstarch. Pour the milk into the sauce pan and set the heat to medium. Heat and stir constantly until the mixture begins to boil. Turn the heat down and continue stirring until it gets thick– about one minute. Take about a half-cup of the hot pudding and add it to the beaten egg yolks and stir immediately. Once combined, pour the egg mixture into the pudding and turn the heat up a little stirring constantly until it starts to boil again. Turn the heat to low and cook for two minutes. Stir in the vanilla. Immediately place a piece of waxed paper or plastic wrap directly on the pudding so it doesn't form a skin and let it cool to room temperature. Chill in refrigerator. This recipe will make about a dozen four-inch eclairs.

For the Pastry:

1 cup water

1 stick unsalted butter

1/4 teaspoon salt

1 cup all-purpose flour mixed with
1 tablespoon sugar

4 large eggs

Bring the water, butter and salt to a boil. Remove from heat. Quickly stir in the flour all at once and beat until the mixture doesn't stick to the sides of the pan. It will be sort of dry. Let cool for about fifteen minutes. Add the eggs one at a time stirring after each addition and well combined. Beat the mixture until it is nice and silky smooth. Using two wooden spoons lay out the dough in about a four by two-inch wide strip on a greased baking sheet. Shape them with the spoons making them fairly rectangular and flat on top. You can also use parchment paper instead of grease, but it will be moving all around unless you adhere with a bit of dough on the corners. Allow about three inches apart on the shells. Preheat oven to 450 degrees and bake them for about fifteen minutes; reduce the heat to 325 degrees for another twenty minutes. When you turn down the oven, open the door and make a stab on the end of each éclair to let out any steam and moisture. When fully baked they should be golden brown. Turn off the oven and let them sit and dry. Not all the pastries will be perfect– some will have holes on the bottom. These probably can't be filled but use them instead for a strawberry shortcake base with strawberries and whipped cream.

Once the pastries are cool, slice them and fill with the chilled custard. Spread the top with chocolate frosting, cool in the fridge, and serve cold.

For the Frosting:

2 squares semi-sweet chocolate for baking
2 tablespoons soft butter
1 teaspoon vanilla extract
1 cup confectioners' sugar, more or less
Water

In a small saucepan, melt the chocolate squares with the butter and the vanilla over low heat. Once melted, stir in the confectioner's sugar. Add more sugar if too thin and add a bit of water if too thick. You want this to be spreadable, but not pourable.

Christmas at the Ricci house was always special. Everyone in the family pitched in to decorate the house. Dad did the outdoor lights and decorations, and we kids took turns decking the other rooms. Trimming the Christmas tree was one thing the entire family took part in.

I remember a particular Christmas season back in '59. About a month before Christmas, we went up into the attic and started pulling down boxes and boxes of Christmas stuff. My brothers and I volunteered to put up the manger and mom reluctantly agreed. We rummaged through the boxes and finally came across the old rickety wooden manger and the figurines. We got some straw from the box and began to assemble everything. Once the manger was in place, we unwrapped all the figurines and began placing them in their positions. Baby Jesus was first, then Mary, and then the wise men. I unwrapped Joseph and stuck him down next to a camel. My brother Richard grabbed him and said, "He belongs next to the donkey, not the camel." I grabbed him once again and replaced him back by the camel. "This is where he was last year," I commented. Well, after another disagreeing snide remark, he once again yanked Joseph and held him up over his head. "Donkey!" my brother shouted! "Camel!" I shouted back, and with that, I grabbed Joseph out of my brother's hand. Just then the Joseph figurine took flight, careening across the living room floor and landing under the sectional. I raced over to the couch and ran my hand under the fringe and pulled out Joseph. He was headless. "Oh, my God. Look what you went and done," I shouted. "I didn't do it. You did," he shot back. "Mom is gonna be soooo mad," he yelled.

I rushed back to take another peek under the couch and his head was nowhere to be found. "It's gone," I said. Rich skidded over to the couch and looked for himself. "Yep! Gone, all right! What are we gonna do?" I finally calmed down enough to think and came up with a plan. I ran upstairs and grabbed my GI Joe doll, got out my Boy Scout hunting knife, and sliced off Joe's head. I ran back downstairs and went into the kitchen utensil drawer and found the DUCO cement. "He'll be as good as new," I said, while cementing the new head onto Joseph's shoulders. "He doesn't look anything like Joseph," Richard snarled. "Joseph has a towel on his head."

"Oh, you're right. Hold out your T-shirt." Before Richard could object, I grabbed the scissors and snipped a piece of my brother's shirt and wrapped it up like a towel. After gluing the ends together, I placed it on Joseph's head. "Hey, that's pretty good," he said, "but didn't he have a beard?"

The wheels were turning once again, so once again I took the scissors and without him even knowing I grabbed Richard's hair and snipped off a chunk. Richie had the nicest curly black hair, so it easily substituted as Joseph's beard.

I carefully fashioned a nice beard, glued it onto Joseph's face, and set Joseph back down next to the camel near the baby Jesus. Once all the other people and animals were positioned, it was hardly noticeable that anything was ever wrong with Joseph. Well, it went unnoticed for about two weeks. Mom was dusting when she got a close look at the imposter standing next to baby Jesus. She wasn't one to curse, but after pulling me and my brother by the ears and leading us to the scene of the crime yelled, "What the $#$@#@ did you do to Joseph?"

Since we were caught, I had to come clean. "We made him into G.I. Joseph, the warrior," I proclaimed. Mom wasn't amused in the slightest. "You will forfeit your allowance for the next two weeks and buy another Joseph. Do you hear?" I agreed and the matter was dropped. That is, it was dropped until two months later when mom was re-arranging the furniture in the living room and came across the decapitated head. She cornered me near the table and held out two fists then asked me to choose one. I thought I was getting a surprise of some sort. I picked the right hand and she opened it up to reveal the true Joseph's head. Then she opened the other hand to reveal a bottle of LePage's glue. "You march your little ass up into the attic and find your butchered G.I. Joseph and fix him."

Needless to say, I never again volunteered to put up another Christmas manger scene.

As you might imagine, with as large a family as we had, individual birthdays weren't very special. We did get a gift or two and maybe a card from a godmother or god father, but for the most part, a birthday was just another day.

I remember my twelfth birthday vividly because of my cake. Let me explain. About a week before my birthday in July, I begged my mom to let me have a birthday party and invite about five of my friends. Mom was reluctant but said okay. I wasn't the sweet, innocent brother to my older sisters as you can imagine, mainly because I was always stealing their toys and taking them apart. A few times, they would find their talking dolls without any voices, or their walking dolls unable to take another step. My fascination with mechanics took a toll on any toy that moved, spoke, rolled, or beeped. I was especially cruel to my older sister Rene, whose record player would fall prey to my inquisitive mind. One day she pulled her little suitcase player out of the closet to play some 45 records with two of her school friends. Upon opening up the lid, she was shocked to find a small box containing a motor, eight springs, fourteen screws, an idler wheel, and three tubes. As expected, she flew into a rage and started yelling obscenities. One of her girlfriends then mentioned a way for her to get even.

Mom had given my sister $8 and instructed her to go to the bakery for a half a sheet cake for my birthday party. The following Saturday, my friends arrived. The dining room was decorated with streamers and balloons and everyone was seated at the table. My sister Rene, carrying the cake, started singing "Happy Birthday" from the kitchen and everyone joined in. As she put the cake on the table, halfway through the verse, everyone just stopped singing and stared.

In script as big as the cake would allow was the message, *ENJOY YOUR 12TH BIRTHDAY … SORRY IT WILL BE YOUR LAST.*

I won't describe my punishment, but luckily, I didn't die.

Speaking of birthdays, I want to share a memory of a really sweet neighbor of ours named Brian. Brian was the first person with Down Syndrome I had ever met. He was extremely lovable—a bit on the large size, and awfully friendly. He was physically about 14 years old but had the mental capacity of a seven-year-old. He would frequently wander across the street with no shoes on when he saw someone he knew in our yard. We would let him sit at the picnic table and he would just smile and repeat the same two or three sentences. This one time he came over he just kept saying, "Bri … new shoes." Of course, he didn't have on any shoes, so we were a little confused. Finally, his mom, Rita, wandered over to fetch him and we asked her what he meant. Well, it was his birthday and all he wanted was a new pair of shoes. This was highly unusual as everyone thought he hated shoes. Still, he kept repeating "New shoes, Bri… new shoes."

Rita finally dragged him back home, but not before inviting all of us over for a small birthday celebration that evening. Rita made a homemade vanilla cake which had the most delicious creamy whipped cream frosting I have ever had. My sister Mare cornered Rita later that evening and scribbled the recipe on a scrap of paper. Years later, I found that recipe and it brought back such great memories of Brian that I thought I would share it here.

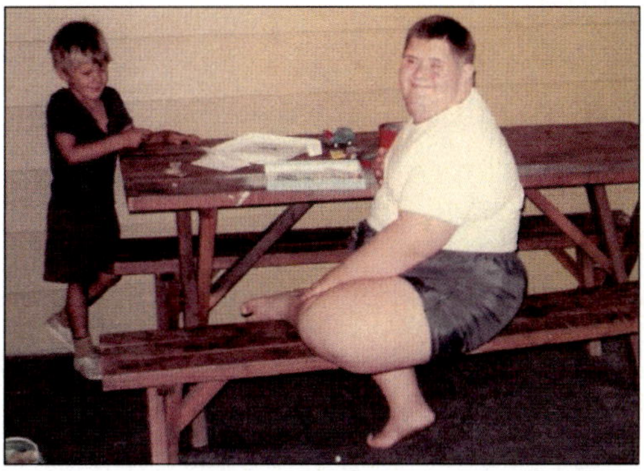

RITA PONDRAC'S HAPPY BIRTHDAY FLUFFY WHIPPED CREAM FROSTING

1-1/2 cups whole milk
6 tablespoons flour
1 stick softened butter
12 tablespoons Crisco shortening
1 cup sugar
3-4 teaspoons vanilla

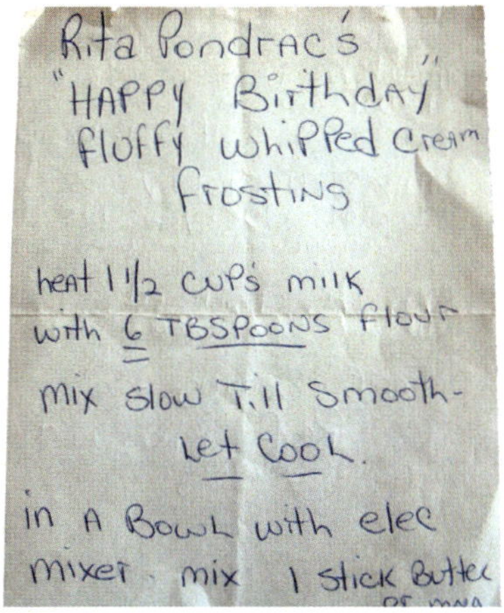

Rita Pondrac's
"Happy Birthday"
fluffy whipped cream
frosting

heat 1 1/2 cups milk
with 6 TBSpoons flour
mix slow Till Smooth-
let Cook.
in A Bowl with elec
mixer mix 1 stick Butter

Heat the milk in a medium-sized saucepan. Add the flour and stir until combined. Cook until the mixture thickens and gets smooth. Use an electric mixer to beat the stick of butter with the sugar, the shortening, and the vanilla until smooth. Add the milk mixture to the butter mixture a little at a time and beat until fluffy. Refrigerate before using. This will frost an 8" layer cake.

I'm sure anyone reading this book has realized that the smartphone, tablet, Gameboy, and many other devices are keeping many people from interacting with each other. I think it's becoming an epidemic of sorts. Two years ago, I spent my birthday vacationing in Punta Cana in the Dominican Republic. I saved and saved and finally booked one of those all-inclusive resorts on the beach. The place was amazing—clean, tropical, friendly, and free flowing food from morning to night. It truly was a paradise. One morning I walked from my hotel room down a few long corridors, passing more rooms to finally come upon a long row of park benches. There was an entire family of seven sitting next to each other. At first, I didn't give them so much as a glance. Then suddenly I had to double back and take a closer look. Every one of them had a cell phone plastered to his or her face. I stood there for what seemed like fifteen minutes and no one moved a muscle except for their swiping or tapping fingers. As I walked away, I thought how sad this was. Here is this family of seven who probably spent a small fortune to travel all the way from wherever to come to this island paradise with balmy summer breezes blowing, the smell of tropical plants all around, and perhaps a dozen adventurous things to be doing here in Eden. And they were all staring into their phones. As I thought more and more while walking to the dining area, I realized I wanted to double back and just snatch each and every one of those phones away and tell them to go enjoy this beautiful day and all it had to offer.

I sat at my table in the dining room and noticed it wasn't just that family but so many others. After getting served a glass of water and coffee, I got up and walked around to the many serving stations to select my breakfast foods. I approached this woman from behind and stood there waiting to place my order with the cook. As I got closer, I noticed that she was gabbing on her phone. Of course, she wasn't paying any attention to anyone but herself and her conversation was being broadcast to everyone within thirty feet of her. After a couple of minutes of eavesdropping, I wanted to just push her out of my way, but that would have been too harsh. I peered around to her face and motioned with my hand to let me by so I could get to the counter. She just kept on gabbing and gave me a snotty look. That's when I surmised that she was talking with her teenage daughter who was sitting just ten feet away. Oh my GOD! Has the world gotten so lazy that the daughter has to phone in her breakfast order to her mother just ten feet away from her? Have we allowed the cell phone to completely take away our ability to communicate with humans on a personal level?

After that trip, I began to take notice of this scenario happening just about everywhere—an elderly couple in Denny's sitting right across from one another in dead silence except for the tap-tap-tap of their tiny keyboards; and people wandering around the aisles of Costco, ignoring how their cart is right in the middle of the aisle while they tell their friend about the awful nail salon experience they had the day before.

I guess the world is changing and the convenience of these devices is also eating away at the very bond that we took so long to create among friends, families, and relatives. Sure, these phones are necessary, and convenient, but there are times when they just are plain annoying. So, there is my rant and rave for the day. If after reading this you might think twice about just talking to your partner, spouse, or family member in person instead of texting them sitting right next to you, then this rant might have served its purpose. Remember, you won't be able to text them when they are dead and gone.

We were one of the first families on our block to get a television set. It was a huge cabinet standing about five feet high and the picture screen was not more than ten inches around. There it sat in the living room with a gizmo on top—two long antenna rods with tin foil wrapped around them. After school, we would rush home just in time to tune in to *American Bandstand* and the *Donna Reed Show*. Of course, rules had to be set down and if there was homework to do, that had to be done before watching any television. Dad wasn't around too much as he kept at least three jobs; but when he was home, the set had to be tuned to a western. In September 1955, John Wayne introduced the nation to a show called *Gunsmoke*. He wasn't in it, but if he endorsed it, Dad knew it had to be good.

Well, the swinging doors from the Long Branch Saloon never stopped swinging in our house, and that show only led us to wander further west to the Ponderosa with *Bonanza* after that. The good thing about us having to sit through boring westerns was that we kids didn't get bombarded with hundreds of ads for sugary cereals, Popeye-shaped pasta, or Jetsons candy sprockets. Advertisers knew that the audience determined the success of their products and so it was mostly on Saturday morning, while the kids were glued to the set, that they hawked their vast assortment of what my mother called "garbage."

I'm not sure whether it was a blessing to be dragged along while your mother and older sisters did the weekly grocery shopping. For one thing, we kids never got "just anything we wanted." If we cried for something we were just told to "Shut up or I'll stick you in the car in the parking lot until we're finished." That idea, of course, would never fly today.

Mom was very frugal with the weekly grocery budget. She planned meals, cut coupons and intently watched sale ads. Every dollar was accounted for and there was not much left over for frivolous "garbage."

One saving grace for our family was the "Jewel Tea Company." We found out about this company from a neighbor and after a few initial deliveries, Tony the "Jewel Tea Guy" as we called him became our very best friend. Tony would arrive once a week around 4:30 pm just as we kids were getting home from school. Tony would pull up, blow the horn twice, then drag in metal cases of everything from clothing to kitchen gadgets. He would bring a catalog of next week's specials and leave it for us to look at. Because soda was too expensive, mom used to let us get beverage syrup from Tony. These were little clear, "bear-shaped" bottles filled with thick orange, cherry, strawberry, or lime-flavored drink syrup. The jar actually doubled as a bank once it was emptied. Each jar made about twenty-five glasses of fruit-flavored beverage. Aside from the cheap shirts and pants mom would buy us, she also let us have a package of oatmeal raisin cookies. These cookies were fresh, soft, and gooey and came wrapped in a package of two, just right for after-school snacks. Since they were only a quarter mom said they were even cheaper than making them from scratch. I've tried many times to duplicate those cookies, but mine always turned out too hard and crusty. Finally, I found the recipe that my oldest sister, Celia, had given me a long time ago. I think it's time I shared it. This recipe makes about five dozen oatmeal raisin cookies, guaranteed to come out soft and chewy.

SISTER CELIA GIGLIO'S
GOLDEN BLOSSOM HONEY OATMEAL RAISIN COOKIES

2 sticks salted butter
3/4 cup honey
3/4 cup light brown sugar
1 egg
1/2 teaspoon vanilla
1/4 teaspoon baking soda
1-3/4 cups all-purpose flour
1-1/2 cups walnuts
1/2 cup sweetened shredded coconut
2-2/3 cups old fashioned oatmeal
1-1/2 cups raisins

My cat, Mufunzarelli, loved showing off.

Preheat oven to 350 degrees. Cream together the butter, honey, and brown sugar until smooth. Beat the egg and vanilla and add to the butter mixture. Add the flour, baking soda, oats, walnuts, raisins, and the coconut and mix until combined. Drop by rounded teaspoon onto an ungreased cookie sheet and bake for eight to ten minutes or just lightly browned.

Living in the 1960s was turbulent. I was in my teens and like many others, I went through the "changes." My acne was awful. My temper was short, along with my stature. I never did grow above five-foot-five. I was rebellious. I often complained about having so many siblings (there were nine of us). For a short time, I also lived in a fantasy world. I imagined having a sweet, loving sister like Judy Jetson (from the space-aged cartoon) or a playmate like Flipper (the dolphin) instead of the family members with whom I got stuck.

I imagined having a really cool aunt like Jeannie who could pop out of a bottle anytime I needed her to replace my worn out Keds sneakers. Of course, in my fantasy, if I ever got into some serious trouble, I would just summon up "Scotty" to beam me over to my grandmother's house in Jersey City where I could be safe.

Granted, my mom was no Donna Reed or Harriet Nelson, and my dad was not a "Paw" like Andy Griffith was to Opie, but we did have

one thing even those TV characters had and that was love. When I was sad, Mom would show her love by making me my favorite meal: Swanson's Chicken TV dinner, the one with the little cranberry crumble dessert side dish. They were all of 97 cents back then, a bargain, and since my mom didn't do much cooking, this was her go-to meal.

Today I am not much of a deep-fried chicken lover, but I do enjoy a simple chicken-fried chicken dinner. The following recipe isn't so much fried as it is baked, which is actually better because it is lower in fat than the actual chicken "fried" chicken but equally as tasty. Enjoy!

CHICKEN FRIED CHICKEN

3 very thick skinless chicken breasts
1 cup Italian seasoned breadcrumbs
1 cup unseasoned Panko breadcrumbs
2 eggs
Flour
1-2 teaspoons Bell's poultry seasoning

For the Gravy:

1/2 stick butter
3/4 cup flour
3/4 cup evaporated milk
2-1/2 cups whole milk
Fresh ground black pepper
Pinch of paprika
Pinch of salt

Rinse the chicken breasts in cool water and pat dry with paper towels. Cut each one in half and place each piece between two pieces of waxed paper or plastic wrap. Pound the cutlets to tenderize them.

Preheat the oven to 350 degrees.

Mix the flour and seasoning together in a flat dish.

Mix the two types of breadcrumbs together and place in another flat dish.

Lightly scramble the eggs in a shallow bowl. Dip the cutlet into the egg and then into the flour, then back into the egg. Then, coat both sides with the breadcrumbs, pushing lightly on the chicken to secure the crumbs. Prepare all the breast halves this way.

In a large glass or metal baking dish, pour a small amount of vegetable oil and coat the bottom. Place the coated chicken pieces in the dish. Cover with aluminum foil and bake for about twenty minutes. Remove foil and check for pinkness in the center. You want them to have a slight pink tint or they will be over-baked and dry. Continue baking without the foil until they are done. Remove from the dish and place on a dish in a warm place. You can lower the oven to about 200 degrees and keep the chicken in the oven (foil wrapped) until ready to serve.

Prepare the gravy by scraping all the drippings from the baking pan into a small pot. Add the butter and melt slowly while stirring. Add the flour and create a rue by stirring and cooking slowly with a metal whisk until the mixture begins to bubble. Add the milks gradually while whisking constantly. The gravy will thicken as it cooks. Once all the milk is added, add the spices to taste. Pour over chicken just before serving. This makes about six servings.

Boy, was I surprised to learn that not all living room furniture comes with plastic coverings. Being from an Italian family our furniture was covered with this clear sticky hard plastic and it was really uncomfortable to sit on. It was hot and sweaty in the summer, and cold and clammy in the winter. I feel as if I were tricked when I went to visit my Jewish friend Levi at his house and his furniture was soft and velvet and a pleasure to sit on. Apparently, plastic coverings were an Italian thing. So were some of the bathroom towels. We were always told not to the "good towels" as they were for the "guests". So, the family got to use the ripped up, holy ones and strangers got to pamper themselves with the nice soft plush ones. I began to notice that there was also a whole brand-new set of fancy "special" dishes that were only for guests, and expensive smelly Parisian soap that was also put out only for guests. I felt cheated! I would have accepted all of these atrocities except that our family... never ever had guests.

WHAT KIND OF WINE?

Whatever your nationality is, at one time you probably had to choose a wine to go with dinner selections. For some people it's quite the science, while others just drink what they are given and don't care one way or the other. Here are some of my educated suggestions as to what wine to serve with what dish. Mind you, this is not gospel, as one's personal taste is what matters in the end.

White wines such as Moscato, Riesling, Pinot Grigio, Chardonnay, Sauvignon Blanc, and Chablis go best with chicken or pork dishes. For a richer sauce, try a sweeter rather than drier blend.

Cherry and plum and sweeter Riesling and Moscato wines go well with Chinese food, lamb, and some pork dishes.

Chianti, Cabernet, Malbec, and Montepulciano are best served with pasta, roast beef, steak, and burgers, as well as with desserts that contain chocolate.

Refosco wines are mostly dessert wines. This ruby red sweet wine produced in the Veneto region of Italy goes well with any Italian dessert like cannoli, tiramisu, tortoni, or pasticotti pastries.

Pinot Noir and Merlot are nice lighter red wines that pair well with dishes containing beef or red pasta dishes.

Shiraz goes well with pork, ribs, Mexican, and Indian foods.

Zinfandel is the idea pairing for pork, chicken, and some rice dishes.

Sometime way back in the early 1960s we moved. Our once described two-story luxury mansion with radiator heat had finally become even too small for our ever-growing family. Dad moved us into the newest fad in architectural buildings; a one-story ranch in a so-called bedroom community in central New Jersey. It had four bedrooms and one-and-a-half baths and a decent back yard to play in, grow vegetables in, and even room enough for a pool and BBQ pit.

So, I wasn't surprised when I arrived home from school one day, walked from the bus stop to our driveway, only to find it filled with a ton of red bricks. My first thought was that our dad was going to build us boys the biggest, neatest play-fort a person ever did see. Nope! Well, after spending the next four hours hauling the bricks to the back yard, nine pieces at a time in a broken-down old wheelbarrow, I realized it was going to be a new barbecue pit.

From the next Saturday, on through the next 16 Saturdays, it started taking shape in the back yard. To this day, I hope I never see another trough of mortar. I must admit we had some incredible and great backyard picnics with the help of that idol centerpiece, the BBQ pit.

My mom was a saint. Ask anyone who knew her growing up and they would all say the same. Mom wasn't just our matriarch, but she was the proverbial glue that held the family together. When my dad died in 1965, she was left to raise the brood and she did a mighty good job of it. As the oldest children grew up, got married and left the nest, the grandkids started coming. And they kept on coming. At one point she just stopped counting. One of my fondest memories of mom was when she would retire for the evening, she would spend at least a half an hour writing in her diary. She would write the names of the kids she had interacted with that day and what they did... even if it wasn't anything earth shattering, she would jot something down. If they learned a new skill, it was recorded. If they got into mischief, it was scribbled in. If someone had a birthday it was noted. Whenever she gave one kid even the smallest gift, she made mention of it. She also wrote about every trip and adventure she ever went on.

One Mother's Day, we took her out to dinner to a small Italian restaurant in New Hope, Pennsylvania called "Mothers". As was our usual custom, any and all of the family was welcome to tag along. This Sunday there were twelve adults and fourteen kids. Once all the initial seating commotion was over, we all got menus and the waitress took our orders. Mom pointed out a dish called Pancetta Con Spaghettini. Mom knew very little Italian and we kids knew even less. I asked the waitress who looked like she just got out of junior high school, what the Pancetta dish was, and she replied that it was a sort of salty deli ham sautéed in garlic served with pasta and peas. We both ordered it. When our meals came the conversation changed from what kind of laundry detergent gets towels whiter, to food. As each plate was set down in front of someone, there would be the usual Oooo's and Ahhh's from anyone who was watching. "Wow, that smells good." Can I get a taste of that"? Before I knew it, both mine and my Mom's plate were being passed around and when we finally got them back, well, there was just enough for an appetizer. Needless to say, it was a big hit with everyone.

About eight years ago, I acquired my Mom's diaries and they remained in a box in the garage all this time. I finally got around to donating some of my garage junk to my neighbor's yard sale and came across the box. I pulled out one of the diaries and flipped through the pages when I came across my mom's entry from that Sunday. I got a little choked up reading it and decided that I would try to re-create that meal just to relive that wonderful day. I had to substitute some of the ingredients, but I think I hit the ball out of the park with my creation. So, in honor of my mom and her special Mother's Day, here is my recipe for revised Pancetta Con Spaghettini. I substituted sausage for the ham, and fettuccini instead of spaghetti. This recipe takes about a half hour to make and serves 6.

FETTUCCINI CON SALSICCIE

1 16-oz package of fettuccini noodles
4 medium hot or mild sausage links
1 medium onion chopped
1 bag (12 oz) frozen sweet peas
4 medium cloves of garlic minced
Olive oil

Cook the fettuccini al dente and drain. Reserve a cup of the water. Place 2-3 tablespoons of olive oil in a medium sized but deep fry pan. Heat the oil for a few minutes then add the meat from the sausage discarding the casing. With a wooden spoon, chop the sausage into small bite sized pieces and stir occasionally until browned. Remove the sausage to a plate, then add the chopped onion. Cook the onion for about 8 minutes until golden brown stirring occasionally. Add the raw garlic and frozen peas and continue cooking until the peas are thawed. Add the cooked pasta and add enough water to make a light sauce. Serve while hot with a generous topping of grated cheese.

Want an easy and light dessert to go with this meal? Try my Lemon Brownies—a one bowl half an hour prep from start to finish.

LEMON BROWNIES

1 cup all-purpose flour
3/4 cup granulated sugar
1/4 tsp salt
1/4 tsp baking soda
2 eggs
1/4 cup plain yogurt
3 tablespoons canola oil
3 tablespoons of fresh lemon juice
Zest from 1 medium lemon

Preheat the oven to 350 degrees. Place a piece of aluminum foil or parchment paper into a 9"x9" square baking pan leaving enough extra to lift out the cake once baked. You can also use a throwaway pan, but line it with foil or paper as well.

Mix everything in a single bowl stirring until just combined. Pour into the pan and bake for 20 minutes.

Let cool for about 15 minutes and prepare a quick lemon icing:

1 cup of confectioners' sugar
Fresh lemon juice
Zest from 1 medium lemon

Stir in enough lemon juice to make a semi-thick icing. Add zest and stir. Pour over cooled cake and remove the cake to a flat counter to allow the icing to dry a bit. Cut into squares and enjoy.

I love pie. There, I said it! If there was one food I could consume from morning until night and never gain an ounce, it would be pie. My earliest recollection of enjoying pie was when I was around 13 years old.

My usual commute walking home from Public School number 9 was to walk across the bridge over the New Jersey Turnpike and wander down the concrete stairs to the parking lot of the Howard Johnson's at Exit 10. Now, for most people, the name Howard Johnson's conjures up one of the twenty-seven flavors of the most exquisite ice cream on the planet; and mind you, from time to time, I also enjoy a scoop or two of one of my favorites—mint pistachio chocolate chip. But for some reason, I took a liking to their selection of pies over their ice cream. Every season that rolled around would cause a frenzy for the advertising department. For Christmas, a limited edition "Chocolate Peppermint Candy Cane Supreme" would be introduced, along with glossy photos of a winter wonderland surrounded with green, snow-laden fir trees amid a small cabin doused with soft candlelight from the kitchen window. On the small wooden table next to the centerpiece of pine cones shiny glass ornaments, and ribbons sits a whole chocolate peppermint candy cane supreme pie. One piece is already cut with a fork beside it, inviting the next human to come grab it and devour it in seconds. That would be me! For fall came a photo of tall aspens leading down a garden path covered with golden leaves of orange and yellow. In the distance would be a farmhouse and next to it a large red barn. A large picnic table decorated with gourds, pumpkins, and yellow and orange squash sits right outside the large barn door. In the center of the table sits a golden-crusted pumpkin pie with decorated leaves made from pieces of pie crust and baked to a golden brown.

I could go on and on, but the memories of those photos almost always made me give up on the ice cream and go straight for that piece of seasonal pie. To this day I still can't proclaim a favorite, but pumpkin and banana cream pies are certainly at the top of my list.

Here is my recipe for one of the best pumpkin pies you'll ever sink your teeth into. This recipe has a slight variation using apple butter in the mix, but it can be made without.

APPLE BUTTER PUMPKIN PIE

1 15-oz. can of solid pack pumpkin
1/2 teaspoon salt
1/2 cup heavy cream
1/2 teaspoon vanilla extract
2 teaspoons Knox un-flavored gelatin
4 teaspoons cold water
1/2 cup powdered sugar
1/2 cup light brown sugar
1 cup apple butter
3 eggs
1 egg white, beaten

1/4 cup pumpkin spice or gingerbread creamer (half-and-half as alternative)

1/4 cup whole milk

1 tablespoon maple syrup

1 teaspoon maple extract

3/4 teaspoon nutmeg

3/4 teaspoon ginger

1 teaspoon cinnamon

1/8 teaspoon cloves

You can use a pre-made frozen deep 9-inch pie crust. Defrost to room temperature, then brush the bottom and sides with the beaten egg white.

Preheat the oven to 450 degrees.

Prick holes in the crust with a fork all around bottom and sides. Pre-bake for ten minutes. Cool.

Combine all the ingredients and mix thoroughly. Pour into prepared pie crust. Bake on the center rack for fifteen minutes then lower the oven temp to 350 degrees. Bake for an additional thirty-five minutes. Check with the tip of a knife in the center for doneness. The knife should come out clean. Remove from oven and let cool to room temperature. Cool the pie in refrigerator until ready to serve.

For whipped cream, make sure the beaters and the metal or glass bowl are clean and cold.

Place the cold water into a small shallow cup. Sprinkle the unflavored gelatin on the water and let it sit for a minute or two until it becomes soft. Heat in a microwave for five seconds and let cool. Pour a half-pint of heavy cream in a deep, narrow, chilled bowl. Add three-quarters teaspoon of vanilla extract and beat on medium until soft peaks form. Add a half-cup of powdered sugar and slowly combine while beating. Pour the cooled gelatin into the cream and whip until the mixture gets thick. Keep chilled until serving. This whipped cream will keep for a good five hours without wilting – even without refrigeration.

Everyone I know rants and raves about the good ol' days. I would often hear my older siblings say stuff like, "When we were kids…" and then they'd go on to talk about the glory of growing up without the aid of seat belts or dual passenger side air bags, ingesting dirt, or riding your bike without so much as a baseball cap to keep you safe if you were run over by a truck. True, we didn't think about how smoking could kill us, or eating bacon could shorten a life by twenty years. We didn't give much thought about how much sugar we consumed in a day or if downing an eight-ounce T-bone three times a week would lead to a person not being around at age 70.

We drank water from the tap and snuck that wad of bubble gum back in our mouths from the bottom of the kitchen table after eating, never once thinking that there were cooties swarming all over it. There was always a pot of coffee ready to be consumed at our house, morning, noon, or night, and no one said, "Hey you won't be able to sleep tonight," ever!

There are always those who will say that research has proven that eating more green stuff than red stuff will do wonders for the mind and body, or that you should trade that second beer for another eight ounces of filtered water. But there is always an extreme to everything. I don't want to be that person who replaces two over-easy eggs, three slices of bacon, dripping with grease, and two slices of good old-fashioned white toast for a large bowl of bitter tasting kale with some grain called quinoa or sorghum. By the way, that last one is used to feed livestock and make bio-fuels. Ugh!

Eating should be pleasurable. Eating with people you love and people who love you should be even more pleasurable. Whenever we have guests over for dinner, I try to serve good old-fashioned, belly-stuffing food that people will want to remember, not because they spent the following twelve hours on the toilet trying to forget what they ate and why. Some of our friends are great cooks and go way above and beyond to impress. Some just buy everything from the take-out menu of a local market or a nearby drive-through restaurant. I like to think I am a little of both. Some days I feel like being some crazed chemistry professor in the kitchen and pulling out all the stops to create masterpieces. Some days I feel like letting the guys at the local deli dictate what I might have for dinner that night. Just to be clear, some days I do both, like making a simply elegant meal by doing almost no hard work at all. The following dish is one of those that I hope you too will find easy and extremely rewarding for those loved ones sitting down at your dinner table.

CHICKEN MARSALA

4 chicken breasts, trimmed of all fat

Marsala wine, dry and sweet variety (NOTE: do not use cooking sherry)

1-1/2 teaspoon dried oregano (I like using Mediterranean style)

1/8 cup or more olive oil

1/4-1/2 stick butter, to start

1/2-1 cup flour

1/4 teaspoon salt

1-2 cups sliced mushrooms

1 small can of chicken broth, low sodium

1 medium-sized lemon

Cut each chicken breast in half and place the halves between two sheets of waxed paper or plastic wrap. Tenderize with a mallet. You may find that higher quantities of ingredients listed are needed, depending on how thick the chicken breasts are. This will make about eight pieces. Mix the oregano, salt, and flour together on a flat dish. Press each breast half into the flour and coat generously. Heat some oil and butter (about four tablespoons each to start) in a Teflon-coated pan on medium low. Brown each of the chicken pieces on both sides. They don't need to be completely cooked yet, just browned. Place the cooked pieces on a plate, cover with foil, and keep them in a warmed oven. Pour about

1-1/2 cups of marsala wine into the pan and use a whisk to mix with the chicken drippings. Add the mushrooms, the chicken broth, and the juice of a medium lemon. Stir using medium heat until the mushrooms are softened and tender. Add the chicken pieces, cover each one with some gravy, and let them warm up and cook. Check the middle of the breasts for pinkness. Very slight pink is okay; they will be nice and juicy. If there isn't enough gravy, you can make more. In a small pot add a half to one can of low-sodium chicken broth, one cup marsala wine, and two to three tablespoons of corn starch. Heat over medium heat until thickened. Add it to the chicken in the fry pan. Once there is enough gravy to cover all the pieces, cover the pan and cook until the chicken pieces are just slightly pink in the center. Serve with rice, noodles, or steamed vegetables. Place a little sauce over each breast and top with a thin slice of lemon and a little bit of parsley for color. The recipe serves eight.

A lot of Italian traditions go by the wayside because parents often don't learn about them from their own parents in order to pass them down to their kids. Such is the legend of Befana. I can remember seeing a witch doll hanging in my grandmother's kitchen when I was a kid. Gram told me she was the Kitchen Witch who was supposed to "Watch the pot doesn't boil over." I didn't give it another thought. While walking through one of the many tourist traps in Rome, I came across the Kitchen Witch doll again. The salesman told me, in broken English, that it was Befana, like Babbo Natale. I surmised that she was supposed to be Italy's version of Santa Claus.

Once stateside, I did a little digging and found out the real story. In Italy, the children celebrate Christmas the same as in the United States, but they celebrate it on a different day—January 6, which is the evening of Epiphany.

According to legend, this was the night that

the three kings offered their gifts of gold, frankincense, and myrrh to the newborn Christ child. Bafana's story begins at the time of the birth of Christ. The story says that the three kings journeyed through Italy on their way to Bethlehem and they stopped to ask directions of an old woman sweeping out her cottage. After she directed them towards Bethlehem, they then invited her to join them in their search for the Christ child and to bring him gifts. "I can't," she snapped. "I'm too busy with chores."

So, the three men moved on and the old woman went back to her task. After a while, she thought that since she had no children of her own and she was quite lonely, she would go after all. She quickly packed a large bag with goodies for the child, took the broom, and started after the caravan. After a while, she got terribly lost, and she never did find the caravan or reach Bethlehem. Yet, the story relates that she wandered around and never gave up her search, even after all these centuries. Whenever she comes to a house where there is a child, she drops in to see if it might be the one she seeks. It never is, but she leaves a gift anyway. In Befana's legend, she realizes over all those years that her searching had not been in vain and that the Christ child can be found in all of God's children. The children of Italy still believe in Befana, and just as the children of America believe in Santa, they leave Befana milk and biscotti in hopes that she will not pass by their house without leaving gifts. Here is one of my favorite recipes for Italian biscotti. Enjoy!

SISTER JUDY TICE'S ITALIAN BISCOTTI

3 cups all-purpose flour

3 teaspoons baking powder

1 cup sugar

1 stick margarine

1 cup crushed almonds or walnuts

1 teaspoon almond extract (use if adding almonds to the dough)

1 teaspoon Anise extract (use if adding walnuts to the dough)

1 teaspoon vanilla extract

3 large eggs

Optional: 3/4 cup mini semi-sweet chocolate morsels

Beat the margarine first and then add the extracts and the eggs. Beat this mixture until smooth and yellow. Gradually add the flour, baking powder, and nuts. Take the dough out of the bowl and place on a floured surface. Add the chocolate morsels if you are using them.

Knead the dough, adding flour until it is no longer sticky. Divide into three parts and shape each one into a rounded loaf. Each should be about 12x3x1 inch thick at the ends. Grease baking pans or use parchment paper and place the loaves in a 350-degree oven for fifteen to twenty minutes, or until lightly brown on top and bottom. Remove from oven and cool about five minutes. Cut the loaves on a slant and place them on edge back onto the baking sheets. Return the baking sheets to the oven to toast, six to eight minutes each side.

Prepare the frosting or glaze for the tops:

2 cups powdered sugar
Milk
1 teaspoon extract (the kind you used in the recipe)

Mix until smooth and lump free. Add more milk if too thick or add more powdered sugar if it's too runny. Then, drizzle the icing over the tops of the cooled biscotti. Depending on the size of the uncut loaves of dough, this recipe should make about 36 biscotti.

Thursday was trash day in our neighborhood. Wednesday, however, was the night my brothers and I would scrounge the alleys and along the side streets for the good garbage. As like many neighborhoods, putting out the trash was just like saying, "Hey, we're throwing out all the stuff our kids outgrew or didn't want anymore."

Sometimes we got lucky and found an old pair of skates, or a slightly used toaster, and sometimes we just found broken lamps and pool sticks.

I managed to come across something one particular Wednesday that I thought was going to be quite a lot of fun. It was a Coleco Electric Football Game. It was still in its original box, which was almost as big as me, sitting there next to the garbage can. I couldn't wait to get it home to try it out even though I didn't even know what kind of game it was. If it had the word "electric" in it, it had to be somewhat exciting.

I knew absolutely nothing about football. I was ashamed to even ask my brothers for fear of being ridiculed so I just decided to read the instruction book and learn by doing. The first snag I hit was that the third, sixth, and ninth pages of the little booklet had so much spilled crap on them that they were difficult to decipher. I learned that a running back had to fumble along the thirty-yard defense line so the linebacker could retreat to throwing a forward pass to the quarterback. All this nonsense about running here and there was just too confusing. I decided just to place all the little guys in a straight line and plug the thing in to see what happened. Once energized, all the men became spastic, jittering all around like they were hit by lightning, spinning around and falling all over one another until they all wound up in a big pile on the other side of the board. It looked like a giant wrestling match, only the six guys on the bottom were already dead from all the weight of those muscle-bulging linebackers. It's no wonder the game was tossed in the trash.

After playing with the toy two or three more times, I got so bored that I decided just to take it apart to see how it worked. There wasn't much in there, just a small motor with a vibrating cam, a few battery parts, and some wiring. What a disappointment. About a half hour later, it was back in the alley next to the garbage can.

FAMILY SHARE: BROTHER-IN-LAW SKIP (LEON) TICE

When I was about 12 years old, my parents would have a bunch of cop friends stop over to the house to play cards and shoot pool. Mom and Dad were friends with all the police because Dad did most of the town's towing jobs. As soon as they arrived, they would all retreat to the basement and get the games started. Being the rambunctious rebel that I was, I would sneak around behind their chairs and "lift" their wallets from their pants pockets without them even noticing. I got to be very good at this. Just before they left for the evening, I would appear with a small box with all their wallets in it and hand them back. The cops were in such disbelief that I was able to rob them blind without them knowing.

One other time a cop named Pete came by the house looking for my dad. I had a real stuffed rattlesnake all coiled up in a small box with its rattler standing straight up in the air. I placed a towel across the top of the box and told Pete I had something great for him in the box. As he opened up the box, I shook the rattle that I had in my pocket to scare the living crap out of him. Needless to say, I thought I was one dead little kid. I laughed so hard, while I started running for my life.

Once I grew up, I inherited my dad's towing service and became a tow truck driver myself. One very late evening I got a call for a tow. Once on the scene, I found a delivery car wrapped around a tree and practically cut in half. The driver survived after falling asleep at the wheel but most of his packages did not. The surrounding streets were strewn with boxes and boxes of chocolate-covered cherries. After getting the car up on the lift, I began to help clean up the mess. I remember just sitting there eating one box after another until I had consumed what seemed like five pounds of candied cherries. You can only imagine where I spent the next couple of days. Yep, on the toilet. To this day, I can't stand to even look at a chocolate-covered cherry.

I'm sure many of you older readers remember getting free gifts inside boxes of laundry detergent. I remember my mother always buying the same brand because she got free towels. With our large brood, we were always going through the towels. We used them to clean up spilled blood when we cut our arms or legs, or when we were changing the oil and couldn't find anything better to wipe up all that dripped petrol in the garage. We used lots of towels to mop up the overflowing septic tank in the basement and when the washing machine refused to hold its allotted amount of sudsy water.

Almost every brand of suds on the grocery store shelf contained some kind of free stuff, including drinking glasses, dinner plates, silverware sets, and plush cotton towels. *BUY ME, COLLECT ALL 12 PIECES*, and *START YOUR SERVICE FOR EIGHT TODAY* were slogans that were plastered all over the boxes in hopes that the consumer would choose their brand. At home, if we broke three water glasses in a week, mom changed detergent brands to get more free ones. If the kids used the everyday silverware to make mud pies in the backyard and accidentally lost one or two forks, mom changed brands again.

Bleach was another story. We used to have bleach delivered to our house. The store brand was too costly, so we found a company that would sell and deliver to us four gallons a week of what we used to call *NO WORRY*. They were just glass gallon jugs, no label, no cautionary words. Just plain old bleach. This stuff was so strong that it got rid of any kid stain, packed on mud and dirt, or engine grease, and it even cleaned a bloody T-shirt.

One day I thought I would take my entire stash of not so "tightie whities" and soak them in this miracle liquid to try and get them white again. I didn't know you were supposed to dilute the stuff. Into a bucket I placed all eleven pairs of briefs and poured a generous amount of *NO WORRY* into the pail. When I came back about two hours later, there was foam and bubbles and steam coming from the top of the pail. I grabbed a stick and gently lifted out my undies and to my surprise realized that they had all completely dissolved into stringy mush. Slight panic set in as I realized that I had no underwear left to wear to school the next day. Fortunately, there was a department store nearby and a short bike ride later arrived home with a new pack of BVDs. They should have named that stuff *Use too much and DEFINITELY WORRY*!

With such a large family our bathroom got quite a lot of use. Our septic tank could only hold so much, so when it backed up into the basement, we knew it was time to have it pumped out. Our house wasn't connected to the city sewer system, so the boys' job was to dig down six feet and across twelve feet to remove the dirt from the lid so that we could save the $50 that it cost for the septic tank company to do that little job. Our reward was chicken cacciatore for dinner, after a hot, steamy shower, of course. This dish is a bit more time consuming than most of the recipes in this cookbook, but don't let that deter you from making it. You will thank me. Just a warning: This meal gets messy to eat, so don't be afraid to get your hands dirty while enjoying this mouth-watering food.

CHICKEN CACCIATORE

1 large whole chicken, cut up, or 8 chicken leg quarters, with thighs

2 large cans of crushed tomatoes or stewed tomatoes

1 jar of prepared marinara sauce

8 oz. sliced mushrooms

1 medium onion, sliced thin

1 large green pepper, cut into small chunks

3 large garlic cloves, sliced fairly thin

2 teaspoons mixed Italian seasoning or substitute equal amounts of thyme, rosemary, basil, and sage

1 cup red table wine (burgundy is great with this recipe)

1 tablespoon paprika

1-2 cups flour in a large brown paper bag

Vegetable oil for frying

Cut up the whole chicken into small pieces and rinse them under cold water. Pat the pieces with a paper towel. Do not remove the skin. In the large brown paper bag, add the flour, paprika, and a teaspoon each of salt and pepper. Add about four pieces of chicken and tighten the bag. Shake the bag to coat the chicken pieces. Place the pieces on a plate or waxed paper and continue coating the remainder of the pieces.

Heat the oil, approximately a half-cup, in a deep cooker pan or small stock pot. Fry the pieces until they are slightly browned on all sides. They do not need to be completely cooked at this time. Remove the pieces and continue frying the remainder of the chicken pieces. Drain the oil and strain it. Set aside about one quarter cup of this oil and discard the rest. Clean out the pot with paper towels and add the one quarter cup of oil back into the pot. Re-heat the oil on low and add the garlic slices. Lightly brown the garlic then add the onion and peppers. Cook until the onion is clear, and the peppers are tender. Add the chicken pieces into the pot, and don't worry if they all don't fit in one layer. Add the cans of tomatoes and the jar of prepared sauce as needed to cover the chicken pieces. Add the wine and mushrooms. Add all the spices at once. Stir the sauce, then cover the pot and let the chicken sauté for about forty minutes on medium heat, stirring every once in a while. Check that the chicken is no longer pink in the center and then add the black olives and cook for an additional ten to fifteen minutes.

Cook the egg noodles al dente. Remove the chicken pieces gently so they don't fall apart and serve over the egg noodles with an abundant amount of sauce on top. Sprinkle a bit of grated cheese if you want. It is perfectly okay to eat the chicken with your hands, just make sure to have plenty of napkins handy. This recipe will serve about eight people and you might still have leftovers.

Here are some handy hints for a perfect chicken cacciatore.

1. Don't burn the chicken.
2. Use small pieces of chicken.
3. Keep the skin on while frying.
4. Use a hearty burgundy or chianti wine.

5. Use a good quality brand of tomatoes and sauce.
6. Invite friends over who don't mind getting their hands messy.
7. Have some Dean Martin or Frank Sinatra music playing.
8. Wipe your hands on your clothes. It's more fun getting a bit messy.
9. Serve a side of thin spaghetti or angel hair instead of egg noodles.
10. Shout this out to your friends and family while eating: "Manga and Buon Appetito!"

I think I mentioned at least once or twice that our family didn't have much money growing up. All of us kids were happy when we found a nickel or dime somewhere on the street, or when aunts or uncles rewarded us with a quarter for doing something nice for them. Paying the utility bills was another story. Dad worked a few jobs and my older sisters worked a little while in school to help out, but we were still living a "paycheck to paycheck life."

I remember mom getting a call from Jersey Central Power and Light Company that the electric bill was way overdue. She would have to make a visit to the office to pay it in person with cash or they would turn out the lights. Luckily or unluckily, I was home from school with a bug of some sort when mom told me to get out of bed and get dressed. I asked what happened and she told me the news. While she rushed around getting things in order, I scrambled under my bed and found my game of Monopoly. I grabbed a few pink bills, and a couple of green bills, a blue one, and a yellow one and stuffed them into my pocket. I quickly ran downstairs, threw on my coat, and rushed out the door after my mother. We walked about three blocks to the bus stop with Mom being awfully quiet. Once on the bus, I asked mom why she was so down. She explained that she didn't have the entire amount of money for the overdue bill and was worried that they wouldn't accept a partial payment. I just stayed quiet and held her hand. We arrived at the JCP&L building and walked into the receptionist's office. The gal there directed us to another office, and we went in and sat down.

After a few minutes, Mr. Rugger came in and laid a copy of our electric bill down on the desk with a huge red stamp on it: Overdue! He showed it to my mom and demanded the full amount of the bill. Mom was a bit shaken by this time and started rummaging through her purse for every crumpled bill she could find. With sadness in her eyes and the beginnings of a tear or two, she explained that this was all she could come up with and that we could possibly have some more money for them on Friday. Mr. Rugger, with a slightly raised voice, demanded every last cent be paid or they would be forced to turn off our power. Mom's reaction to that was one of desperation and fear. Her face turned bright red and she started to cry. She stood up, wiped the tears away with a handkerchief, and ask to be excused to the ladies' room. She told me to stay there and she would be back in a minute or two. Mr. Rugger tried to explain to me that his hands were tied and that this electric bill had been way overdue for months. I got up from my chair and reached into my pocket. First, I pulled out an orange Monopoly card that said, "Bank error in your favor. Collect $200." I reached in again and I pulled out each one of the colored Monopoly bills and placed them on his desk.

"Will this be enough to keep our lights on?" I pleaded. Mr. Rugger reached out, snatched up the bills in his hand, and gazed right into my sincere brown eyes. He kept fumbling with the bills in his hands and didn't speak for what seemed like hours. Finally, he went over to his filing cabinet, opened one of the drawers, and pulled something out. He placed the paper down on the table, stuffed the Monopoly money into the desk drawer, and sat there with his hands folded. He and I didn't say another word. When Mom came back into the room and started to say something, Mr. Rugger got up and said, "Mary, there's been a terrible mistake. This overdue bill isn't yours but belongs to someone else. Your bill is exactly $12, and you have enough money here to satisfy the electric company. Here's your receipt and you are free to go."

Mom was pretty quiet all the way home on the bus and finally she asked me what Mr. Rugger had to say while she was in the restroom. I just said he told me that "Sometimes small miracles happen to good people." I never did tell her about the bank error in our favor.

Most people who know me know that I have an affinity for sweets. I am drawn to cookies like a moth is to a flame. I love pies and cakes and well, just about anything that has a frosting on it. It's a wonder that I don't weigh 500 pounds, but perhaps it's because as I get older, I try to mentally limit my sweets intake. So instead of sitting there with a whole bag of Oreos, I just grab four and a half a glass of milk and convince myself that my craving is gone. Sometimes it works.

One of my favorite snacks is zucchini bread. I have tweaked this recipe a few times and I think this one is a keeper. Mine is more like a dessert—a moist, semi-sweet, flavorful bread that is great for an afternoon snack or an after-dinner dessert served with whipped cream or vanilla ice cream.

ZUCCHINI BREAD

This recipe will make three loaves of bread, approximately 4x8 inches.

Grease and flour three loaf pans (preferably glass). You can cheat and use those throw away foil pans from the dollar store, but generously grease and flour them beforehand.

Preheat the oven to 325 degrees. Try not to overbake.

In a large mixing bowl add:

3 eggs
1/2 cup vegetable oil
1/2 cup unsweetened apple sauce
2 cups sugar
3 cups grated zucchini, skins and all
3 cups all-purpose flour
2 teaspoons vanilla
1 teaspoon baking soda
1/4 teaspoon salt
2 teaspoons ground cinnamon
1/2 teaspoon ground nutmeg
1/2-3/4 cups chopped pecans or walnuts

Mix everything together with a wooden spoon. Don't use a mixer. Just mix until combined.

Fill each of the prepared pans about three-quarters full and bake on the middle rack of the oven. Test for doneness with a toothpick after about thirty-five minutes. Remove from oven and let cool for about a half hour before taking them out of the pan. Cool completely and serve warm.

My dad was the best deal maker there was. If there was a will and a way to get things our family needed, Dad knew how. He knew lots of people and he often bartered for what we needed but couldn't afford. I can remember many a Saturday when rather than being out playing with my friends and cousins, I was whisked away in the early morning hours to spend the day picking vegetables on one of my dad's friend's farm. Knowing now what I didn't when I was growing up, I can appreciate what a great lesson he taught by having us kids work on that farm, instead of being outside building yet another go-kart.

We worked on the Juliano Farm in Lincroft, New Jersey, for many summer weekends. We picked everything from tomatoes to cucumbers, peas, and carrots. Most Saturdays, we worked for about four hours. The deal my father made was that whatever produce we picked we got to keep a bushel or two of that day. That would be our "pay."

Mr. Juliano had three older sons, Vincent, Carmine, and Joseph. They often helped us with carrying the bushels of veggies to the trucks out in the field. Sometimes we would get rides on the farm trucks and tractors and that was always a lot of fun. There's something pleasurable about getting totally filthy from farm dirt spewing up into your face while riding on the back of a tractor. For those many summer and fall months, our evening meals always consisted of the freshest vegetables that we picked and canned. To this day, I still believe that a truly great meal requires serving the freshest vegetables you can get.

OMG! I just remembered that Christmas time is approaching fast, and I haven't started cooking or baking yet. Okay, planning ahead isn't my best attribute, but it does save lots of headaches if you start early on making those cakes and cookie platters. Here is when the freezer comes in handy. If I am planning a party, or a large get-together, I will start weeks ahead of time and make the things that will freeze well. The following cookie recipe is one of them.

RICOTTA (CHRISTMAS) COOKIES

1 stick butter, at room temperature
1-3/4 cups granulated sugar
2 teaspoons vanilla extract (or substitute almond, lemon or orange extract)
2 cups whole milk ricotta cheese
2 large eggs
2 level teaspoons baking soda
1 level teaspoon salt
4 cups all-purpose, unbleached flour

Buttercream Frosting:

1/2 stick softened butter

Note: You can eliminate the butter and just make a white icing

3-4 cups powdered sugar

1/2 teaspoon extract (use the same extract used in the cookie dough)

Milk

Preheat oven to 350 degrees.

In a large mixing bowl, cream together the butter and sugar and mix until very fluffy.

Add the extract, ricotta cheese, and eggs. Mix until combined

In another bowl, mix together the flour, baking soda, and salt and gradually add this to the butter/sugar mixture, mixing well with each addition.

Use parchment paper on a large baking sheet and drop the dough by heaping teaspoonfuls onto the paper, leaving about two inches between each cookie. Bake in the center of the oven for approximately ten minutes, or just until they are slightly browned on the edges. Don't overbake them. Remove from oven and let cool before removing from baking pan. Cool completely before decorating.

Combine all the ingredients for the icing and add the milk as necessary for a nice smooth icing, but not runny. If you wish, separate some icing and tint each with red and green food coloring. Generously frost the cookies. You can use colored sugar, or colored jimmies, but put them on immediately—before the frosting has time to set. Once the frosting is dry to the touch, place them in a plastic container and burp the lid to remove some air. They will keep fresh for about two weeks, or you can now freeze them for about one month. Makes about 36 cookies.

Italian Saying: "I only eat thin spaghetti so I don't get fat."

Growing up in the fifties and sixties was so different from today. We didn't have many of the luxuries kids have today—no iPads, game-boys, or smartphones. We didn't get a TV until I was about seven years old. Even back then there were only a few programs on that we could watch, so we didn't spend an ungodly number of hours in front of the boob tube, as it was called. We spent most of our childhood lives unsupervised, unregulated, and robustly physical. We were always outdoors. I remember being pushed out the door at 8 o'clock in the morning and being told we were not allowed back in the house until after 5 pm. There were only three reasons mom would allow us back inside: 1) if we were bleeding; 2) if we were on fire; and 3) if we were starving. Once the streetlights came on, we rushed home usually just in time for dinner. After washing up and rushing downstairs, I would smell the pot of sauce cooking on the stove and I knew I was in for some good ol'-fashioned Italian food. There were a few times, though, when I was just slightly disappointed. Instead of a pot of spaghetti or rigatoni, there was a pot of polenta. In our house it was known as Italian grits or just plain SLOP! Regardless of what we called it; polenta was served when that's all we had. It was cheap, and it filled our little tummies pretty darn well.

There is no shame in saying that we were a poor family at times—but a loving family always.

POLENTA

6 cups water

2 cups polenta

SUNDAY SAUCE (page 16) or gravy (or substitute a jar of prepared spaghetti sauce)

Bring the water to a boil in a large pot. Lower the heat until the water is just simmering. Slowly pour in the polenta in a steady stream while stirring constantly. Continue to stir until the polenta thickens and pulls away from the sides of the pot. Turn it out into a serving dish and let it cool a bit. Scoop some into individual dishes and top with the hot sauce. Add some grated cheese if you want and serve. Polenta can be used as a side dish for chicken and other meat entrees. This will make about 12 medium servings.

A mysterious letter arrived one day for me from the I.R.S. When I got home from school, my sister handed it to me and asked what I had done to involve the Internal Revenue Service. I couldn't think of anything I could have done or not done to warrant this letter. I started to sweat, and my hands got clammy. I was nervous to say the least. I finally opened the letter and started reading:

"Dear Mr. Ricci,

This letter is to inform you that there is a discrepancy that needs to be cleared up. You are hereby requested to show up at..."

The letter went on to tell me where to go, and whom I should meet and when, but it did not give me anything more about WHY!

"Please bring this letter with you and any important information you deem necessary to validate your claim."

WHAT? I didn't have a claim against the government. I paid my taxes. I never even gambled. "WHAT COULD THEY POSSIBLY WANT ME FOR?" I blurted out. My sister said, "Maybe it's a mistake and they think you are somebody else. The appointment is in two weeks; we'll find out then."

The next two weeks were torture. Every day after school, I came home and took out that damn letter and read it and re-read it, over and over, trying to make some sense of it. I couldn't think of one reason why they wanted to see me in person.

When the day arrived, I took off from school and my older sister pulled up in her little red VW Bug to pick me up. I grabbed my lucky rabbit's foot key chain from its hook on the wall and we left. We drove into the town of Red Bank and parked in front of the Jersey Shore Bank and Trust building. We took the elevator to the second floor and found the offices for the I.R.S. I held the letter in my hand and a bunch of paycheck stubs I had from my one and only job at Borge's Bakery in Hazlet. I was the only one in the room and the receptionist asked my name. I told her who I was, and she told me to sit and wait to be called. Within five minutes, I was told to step into Mr. Grangier's office. My sister wished me good luck. I tugged on my lucky rabbit's foot and walked in. "Please have a seat, Mr. Rice," he said. I corrected him with the pronunciation of my name, and he pointed to the chair.

"There is a discrepancy, Mr. Ricci," he said without looking up from his desk. I didn't say a word but let him continue. "Your math is all wrong," he said. I just said, "Huh," and he went on. "You made a mistake on your income tax form. You subtracted when you should have added," he said. "The government owes you some money," he added and proceeded to show me my mistake on the form.

"I must tell you, sir, that math is not my best subject and I'm sorry for the mistake."

"The mistake is in your favor, Mr. Ricci. Here is a check for $272.55. Please sign this voucher and you may go," he said.

I was in total shock. I never in a hundred years would have guessed that a simple mistake would reward me with all that money. I can't remember what I did with it, but I'm sure it went to a good cause.

I keep my checkbook in a bill holder, right above the hook where I keep my lucky rabbit's foot. I haven't balanced it in over thirty years. I prefer it that way.

Remember me talking about Tony, the Jewel Tea Company guy? Here is another story of how Jewel Tea helped us save Easter.

When I was about 6 years old, I stopped believing in the Easter Bunny. I was also teetering on my faith in some of the other myths such as the Tooth Fairy, forest trolls, and Santa Claus. I still did believe in the power of the human spirit, which for some strange reason always saved the day.

A week before Easter, Mom would pull out a small red change purse she had hidden and sit us kids down at the table to count out the money in the "Easter Miracle Fund," as she called it. Starting right after Christmas, she would put aside a few bucks here and there and tuck them away in that little red purse. Her hopes were that there would be enough by Easter week to get each and every one of us a new outfit to wear to mass on Easter Sunday. As she started dividing up the money, she realized that there just enough money for shoes and nothing else.

"Some of you will just have to wear last year's clothes," she said. I guess she must have forgotten that we were growing kids and that we had already outgrown last year's things. Since I was the oldest of the boys, my clothes were handed down to my middle brother, Pat. Pat in turn passed his clothes down to our youngest brother, Rich. Celia was the oldest of the girls and she did the same with her clothes and everyone wound up with something new to wear. That is, except for me and Celia.

The following day, Tuesday, at exactly 4:30 pm, Tony arrived as always. Tony was always upbeat and funny. He had a strong Brooklyn accent and always talked with his hands.

"Mary," he barked, with his hands outstretched, "I gotta small problem and maybe you can help." Mom asked him what it was, and he explained. "Well, I got this customer over on Leonardville road who has two kids, a 9-year-old boy and a 14-year-old girl. She ordered each of them a really nice set of Easter duds for Sunday and I accidentally ordered two of each instead of one. I know you have a couple of older kids and I was wondering if they could use these outfits, 'cause I can't return 'em. I'll give them to 'ya for a few bucks, whatever you can afford Mary. Whadaya say?"

With that, Tony opened his huge carry case and pulled out a fancy dress and a pair of brown slacks and yellow long-sleeved shirt with tie. Mom just stared at the clothes for a minute and told Tony that she would go and check to see how much money she could spare. She disappeared for a moment and came back holding out $3. Tony grabbed the money and hugged my mother, saying what a great customer she was for saving his neck. As it turned out, the clothes were worth at least five times that amount because we saw them in his catalog.

We did manage to all get new shoes and we did have enough money to get Easter baskets as well. It was one of the best Easters I could ever remember. And speaking of Easter, food always played an important part in making it a special holiday. Dad would make his famous Pizza Gain Pie which included Italian ham, cheese, and an Italian rice. He would bake umpteen loaves of Easter bread with colored eggs baked right in them, and of course a scrumptious ricotta pie for dessert. I want to share both of those recipes with you.

ITALIAN RICOTTA PIE

For the Filling:

15 oz. whole milk ricotta cheese
1 cup sugar
3 eggs
1 teaspoon flour
1 teaspoon almond extract
2 teaspoons orange peel or fresh orange zest
2 teaspoons lemon peel or fresh lemon zest

Mix all the ingredients well and refrigerate until ready to use.

For the Crust:

1 cup all-purpose flour
1/4 teaspoon baking powder
1 teaspoon salt
1 egg
1 cup sugar
1 teaspoon vanilla extract
1 teaspoon orange peel or zest
3-4 tablespoons orange juice
3 tablespoons soft unsalted butter
Optional: 1 beaten egg for egg wash

Sift the flour in a bowl and add the baking powder and salt. In another bowl, using a mixer on medium/low speed, whip the butter, sugar, and the egg until light and fluffy. Beat in the vanilla, orange juice, and orange peel. Use a wooden spoon and add the flour a bit at a time until the dough forms. You can use your hands to combine and smooth out the dough. Wrap in plastic wrap and let it rest for about thirty minutes.

Prepare a 10-inch glass pie pan with Crisco or lard and set aside. Preheat the oven to 350 degrees.

Cut the dough in half. Cut two large sheets of waxed paper and place on the counter.

Roll out one half of the dough between the two sheets of waxed paper to about a 10-inch round. Remove the top piece of waxed paper and flip the dough down inside the prepared glass pie pan. Remove the other piece of waxed paper and press the crust up along the edges of the pie plate. Curl the top edge slightly all around the top to make a small edge.

Roll the rest of the dough out between the sheets of waxed paper, forming another 10-inch round. Remove the top piece of paper and place a small amount of flour on the table or counter. Flip the crust onto the counter and remove the waxed paper. With a pinwheel pizza cutter, cut the entire circle of dough into one-inch strips, starting from one outer edge to the other. The goal is to create a crosshatch pattern.

Fill the pie pan with the ricotta filling and smooth it out. Begin with the longest strip of dough and place it in the center of the ricotta filling. Add the next longest strip onto the pie, leaving about an inch of filling between them, and continue placing them on the left and right until five or six of the horizontal strips are in place. Now, do the same thing vertically and remember to leave at least one inch between the pieces. Use a fork to seal the edges of the strips to the bottom crust layer, all the way around. You can use the beaten egg as an egg wash over each strip and around the edges to give it more of a sheen when baking. Bake in a 350-degree oven for about fifty minutes. Check the crust for browning after a half hour. You can prepare aluminum foil strips to place around the edges if they are browning too much or use a commercial crust ring. Remove the pie and let it cool before placing it in the refrigerator. Sprinkle powdered sugar over the entire pie before serving.

BRAIDED EASTER BREAD

It may seem odd that this next recipe is in a different format than usual, but I would like you to make this bread in the manner as it was taught to me. This recipe will make three large, double-braided bread loaves and four to five small single braided loaves.

... in my younger days—a fancy Easter Bread with almonds

The first thing to do is dye some cooled hard-boiled eggs in nice bright colors. You will need four each for the large loaves and one for each of the small ones. You can use food coloring if you don't have a store-brought coloring kit. Add a tablespoon of white vinegar to one cup of cool water in a shallow mug and add three to four drops of coloring to your desired color and shade. If you have a nice heavy-duty stand mixer, you can use it for this recipe to save some time and cut down the kneading time.

Place two cups of flour in a large mixing bowl. I like using bread flour, but all-purpose flour works just as well. Add two packages of rapid-rise dry yeast, a half-teaspoon of salt, and a half-cup of granulated sugar. Mix well. In a medium saucepan, combine one-and-a-half cups of milk, three-quarters stick of softened unsalted butter, and two tablespoons of Crisco shortening. Heat on low until the Crisco is melted. Remove from heat and add a pinch of salt. Check the mixture with a yeast thermometer. It should be between 105 and 115 degrees. Let it cool if it is too hot. Add one-and-half teaspoons of vanilla extract and one teaspoon of orange peel or zest. Mix well and add it to the flour. Add three medium or large eggs and mix for about two minutes. With the mixer on low speed, add more flour, approximately four cups until a nice soft dough is formed. Using your mixer, or your hands, begin to knead the dough. Add more flour as needed until the dough no longer sticks to the bowl. Turn the dough out onto a floured surface and knead until it becomes smooth and elastic. It is important to knead for about six to eight minutes total by hand, or for at least five minutes in the mixer. Using butter or shortening, grease the bowl and place the dough back into it. Cover with a towel and place in a warm location. Let the dough rise for about two hours.

Once risen, punch the dough back down and split it into four to six equal pieces. Roll the pieces into a rope about one inch thick. Braid two pieces together, crossing over onto itself and then form this into a circle. Pinch the edges together. Place the wreath on a greased cookie sheet. Coat the colored eggs with a little vegetable oil. Place three to four colored eggs under one of the braids of the wreath or place them into the center all together, whichever you prefer. For single loaves, use one longer rope of dough, braid it over itself, and leave a larger portion at the top for the egg to sit in. Note: You can also just skip the colored eggs altogether and make them plain. Place the breads on a parchment lined or greased baking pan. Cover the breads with a large towel and set aside in a warm location to raise again. It will need about forty-five minutes and it should double in bulk. Before baking, brush the top with beaten egg yolk with a bit of water added. Bake in a 375-degree oven for about twenty-five minutes or until they are a nice golden brown. Let the breads cool completely. Decorate with colored icing (powdered sugar, milk, almond or vanilla extract with a drop or two of pastel colorings). Brush the icing on with a pastry brush or just lightly pour it on top while the bread is still slightly warm. You can add colored sprinkles, toasted almond slices, green tinted coconut, or leave them plain with just the colored icing. Get creative with your jimmies.

Here is another of my dad's favorite desserts, which he made and served in the Pizzeria. This recipe is so simple you will make it for Christmas and other holidays as well as Easter. Cassata is a dessert cake and the people of Sicily are famous for their desserts and pastries. Serves 10.

CASSATA ALLA SICILIANA

1 plain pound cake (store brought) I like Sara Lee Brand

24 ounces of whole milk ricotta cheese

2 tablespoons heavy cream

1/4 cup granulated sugar

2 tablespoons of orange juice

1/4 cup of semi-sweet chocolate morsels

1/2 cup of dark rum

4 squares of unsweetened chocolate

1/4 cup butter

3-1/2 cups confectioner's sugar (a one-pound box) sifted

1/2 cup of strong hot coffee (espresso preferred)

1-1/2 teaspoons pure vanilla extract

1/4 cup of finely chopped or diced candied fruits

Cut the ends off the pound cake and then cut the loaf lengthwise into three even layers. In a bowl, mix the ricotta until smooth. Beat in the heavy cream, sugar and orange juice. Fold in the chocolate morsels and the chopped candied fruit. Stir until combined. Place the bottom layer of cake on a tray and sprinkle it all over with the rum. Spread 1/2 of the ricotta filling on this layer. Place the second layer on top, douse with more rum and layer on the rest of the filling. Slice off the rounded top of the last layer to make the loaf look more square. Press the cake layers so the filling reaches out to the edges of the sides. Cover with plastic wrap and chill for 2 hours.

For the frosting:

Melt the chocolate squares with the butter in a small saucepan over very low heat. Once nice and smooth, remove from heat and add the confectioner's sugar, hot coffee, sugar and vanilla extract. Beat it with a wooden spoon until smooth and no lumps remain. The frosting should be fairly thick. Chill the frosting for about an hour. Frost the cake sides and top with a thin layer of chocolate frosting. Place the remainder of the frosting in a plastic bag or piping bag and decorate around the top sides and across the cake with 3 or 4 strips of chocolate icing. At the edges and in the center make some chocolate star shapes as shown in my photo. Chill the cake for at least 2 more hours before serving. You can also add sliced cherries or other chunks of candied fruit for more decoration. Serve with some Spumoni ice cream and espresso coffee.

KITCHEN TIP: For maximum garlic flavor, finely chop the garlic cloves so that every edge gets into the food. For medium garlic flavor, slice the clove razor thin and sauté it until golden brown.

When you are a poor kid with only $3.42 in your piggy bank, and the Remco Advanced Super Dooper Chemistry set that you can't live without costs almost $20, you have to think of ingenious ways to get that kind of money. I found it on the back page of a Huey, Dewey, and Louie comic book. There in giant letters the headline read, "KIDS … Make MONEY Now!"

Naturally I was pinned to the page. All you had to do was sell Mrs. Leyland's Peanut Butter Bits. They came in five different collectors' tins with five brightly colored plastic lids to keep them fresh once opened. Hmm, I thought…no money down, just sell them door-to-door and make $2 on each $5 sale. As you know by now, my math skills sucked, so I quickly filled out the form and ordered 200 cans.

After anxiously waiting for two whole weeks, they finally arrived. Twelve large cases of Mrs. Leyland's Peanut Butter Bits, along with eight boxes of lids sat on the carport when I arrived home from school. I immediately tore into them and opened one up just to taste what they were like. They were really good—kind of butterscotch tasting with a center of real peanut butter, all in a tiny, pillow-shaped candy. I knew I wouldn't have much trouble selling them.

Early Saturday morning, my brothers and I loaded up our trusty wagon with candy and lids and off we went, up and down Richard Street, Jack Street, Susan Street and then Willowbrook Drive. We sold every single can of candy we had in that one afternoon. When we got home, I dumped all the money on my bed and started counting. We had almost $100. Once we exhausted our neighborhood, the sales were fewer and fewer. The houses got further and further apart, and it was a lot harder to lug that wagon loaded down with cans of candy. After about two weeks of selling after school and on weekends, we decided that it was just too much trouble to continue. We decided to split the money and keep the rest of the unsold candy. Three weeks later, we started getting bills in the mail from the company demanding payment for the shipment. My older sisters warned us that we were going to be in a lot of trouble if we didn't pay these people. We ignored them and the twenty or so notices of delinquency we kept getting. Finally, we got a nasty, official looking letter from a law firm. I don't quite remember how the whole thing ended, but I do know that Dad confiscated the money and we were grounded for a whole month. I never did get the chemistry set but what I did get was some terrible stomach aches from eating all the leftover tins of peanut butter bits.

Enjoy this recipe for the most delicious peanut butter pie you ever tasted.

PEANUT BUTTER PIE

1 cup creamy peanut butter

1 cup granulated sugar

1 8-oz. package cream cheese, at room temperature

1 teaspoon vanilla extract

1 cup whipping cream

1 9-inch pre-made graham cracker crust

4 oz. semi-sweet chocolate morsels

3 tablespoons soft butter

In a mixer bowl, cream together the peanut butter, sugar, cream cheese, and vanilla until blended and fluffy. In a separate bowl, whip the heavy cream until soft peaks form. Stir half of the whipped cream into the peanut butter mixture, folding until blended. Continue with the rest of the whipped cream. Pour into the prepared crust. Refrigerate for at least two hours. In a small saucepan, melt the chocolate and butter together. Cool. Drizzle over the top of the peanut butter pie and refrigerate again until firm. Sprinkle cocoa powder over the top before serving, or better yet, melt some peanut butter cups with a bit of heavy cream and serve over the cut slices.

I was one of the fortunate kids in my family who got to go to summer camp four years in a row. Although we lived in Monmouth County, we were permitted to go to Kiddie Keep-Well Camp, which was in Middlesex County in New Jersey.

My first summer there I learned how to swim, how to build a fort out of popsicle sticks, how to administer first aid and how to carve a flute out of bamboo. I also learned what a joy it was not to have six sisters around for three whole weeks. Kiddie Keep-Well Camp was built on rolling hills inside of a state park named Roosevelt Park. There were eight cabins that could hold about twelve kids each. The first three cabins were kind of small and cramped and had just cots and a small footlocker to keep personal stuff in. The first time I went there, I was assigned to the first cabin—number 1. The second year I progressed up the hill a bit to cabin number 2.

The floors creaked, and the cabins had huge window frames without glass. They had screens that closed to keep out the bugs, and then wooden shutters that could be closed in case of heavy rain and winds. On really hot summer days when there was no breeze, the temperature inside that cabin got pretty hot. I think I was around 7 years old when I first started going. I got to spend three weeks away from home, doing nothing but fun stuff from morning to night. We had crafts days on Wednesdays and there were plays on stage on Fridays. We got to swim, fish, camp out, and play lots of games with other kids in the same age group. The mess hall served mostly hot dogs and hamburgers, chili, and French fries. Occasionally we got macaroni and cheese and every second Friday was meatloaf day.

Every afternoon around 12:30 they rang a huge bell in the tower of a building across from the infirmary. All the kids would come running from wherever they were, and we would stand in line for a cup of fresh, from-the-cow milk. Someone would hand you a green Dixie cup and then dip a large ladle into a metal milk jug and pour you out some really cold fresh milk. After you drank the milk, you were free to return to whatever you were doing. They stressed that kids shouldn't miss the milk line for anything. I must admit, their milk was the best tasting, freshest milk I ever drank.

The only thing I really missed during my summers at Kiddie Keep-Well were the home-cooked, sit-down Italian dinners, especially those special Sunday dinners when we served pasta with all the fixings.

I was invited to an informal dinner party and they asked me to bring dessert. My favorite go-to Italian dessert has always been Tiramisu, so I decided to whip one up. Mind you, this isn't something a person can manage in twenty minutes. This dessert is made using sponge cake doused with brandy and coffee, mixed with Italian cream cheese, cocoa, and whipped topping. It was a huge hit at the dinner party and I'm sure you are going to love it too.

I like using a large, clear glass bowl on a pedestal only because this dessert is time consuming and it certainly deserves to be proudly displayed.

TIRAMISU

1 lb. container mascarpone cheese (not cream cheese), at room temperature

4 egg yolks

1/4 cup sweet Marsala wine

1/2 cup sugar

1/4 cup brandy

1 cup heavy whipping cream

20-30 Italian ladyfingers (I prefer the Savoiardi brand)

Semi-sweet or Dutch style cocoa powder

8 oz. almonds, sliced and toasted

You will need a double boiler for this recipe. Beat the egg yolks in a metal or glass bowl and add the sugar. Set the bowl over a pot of simmering hot water and then add the brandy and the wine. Stir constantly for about ten minutes until the egg mixture thickens. Remove from heat and let it cool.

Prepare some very strong coffee (about two cups worth) using an espresso type grind. Let the coffee cool and add two tablespoons of sugar and stir. Whip up the mascarpone cheese and add it into the egg yolk mixture. In a chilled bowl using chilled beaters, whip up the heavy cream until stiff peaks form. Gently fold the whipped cream into the mascarpone cheese mixture. Don't beat the mix; just gently fold in. Pour the cooled coffee into a large pie pan or baking dish.

I like using a large, round glass truffle bowl on a pedestal only because this dessert takes a lot of time and effort and you want to make sure it is seen. If you don't have one on a stand, a plain, clear bowl will do.

Dip each end of the lady fingers into the coffee and let them absorb for a few seconds. Don't make them too soggy. Place them into the bowl either lying down or standing up around the inside of the glass. Continue to add lady fingers to form a single row. Spread a good amount of the cheese mixture on the cookies. Toss some toasted almonds on top of this layer and sprinkle with some unsweetened cocoa powder. Repeat this step for the next two layers, making sure there are no gaps between the cookie layers. You should get about three layers total. Sprinkle the remaining cocoa powder on the top and refrigerate for about four hours. Serve cold. Makes about 12 servings.

If you grew up in the sixties like I did, you probably had a little more freedom to explore as a kid than the kids today do. Back then, it was a less violent world with fewer perverts and fewer unscrupulous people trying to sell drugs or other harmful stuff. Kids were free to wander down unfamiliar roads into abandoned fields and yards where only weeds grew, and creatures crawled.

I remember one day on my way home from school I decided to take a short cut into the woods behind the Route 35 Drive-in Theatre. As I wandered along into the thick woods, I came across something I didn't even know existed in our little town– a dump! I remember it being stinky and smelly but enticing all the more. I walked out onto the heaps of garbage, discarded office furniture, old appliances and mattresses, and broken-down couches. Suddenly I noticed lots and lots of unopened boxes all marked with the letters PNB. There had to be a dozen or more of them, all marked the same, with the same letters printed on them. I searched around for a sharp object to cut the tape with and found a long roofing nail. I grabbed it and started tearing into the first box, all the while was wondering if there was money inside or candy or toys or maybe even tons of baseball cards. What I didn't expect were pens. Yes, thousands and thousands of ball point pens, all stamped with the logo for People's National Bank. I opened the second box and found more pens. I went on to the third. Pens. Boy, what a gyp. Well, about this time I wondered if my family was worrying where the heck I was, so I grabbed about 300 of the cellophane wrapped pens and rushed off to home.

Once I got there, Mom started with the questions, "Where were you? What happened to you?" I opened my bookbag and started pulling out handfuls of pens and told her the story. "Look," I said, "brand new pens. Lots of 'em. I found them in a junk yard behind the drive-in."

Well, Mom, being the skeptical person, queried once more. "What were you doing in a junk yard? Don't you know there are snakes and rats in there? You could have gotten bit! And besides," she continued, "who would be so stupid to throw away hundreds of perfectly good pens?"

"Beats me," I said, "but they were all new and still in wrappers." Mom then grabbed one, tore off the plastic wrap, and started scratching marks on a piece of paper. "Nothing!" She opened another. Dry. And so it went.

"See, I told you, you'll never find anything of value in a junk yard." Boy, was I disappointed. All of these pens and not a single one worked. No wonder the people at the bank threw them out.

I did wander back into that junk yard from time to time after that, and the only good thing I found was a stack of 45 records, brand new, still in their original picture sleeve wrappers. I put them in a suitcase in the attic along with my original 1960s RCA phonograph. Despite what mom said, those picture sleeve records did become valuable. It just took about fifty years for them to do so.

I must take a bit of time here to talk about my home state of New Jersey. Sure, if you mention New Jersey to some, they probably will bring up that awful TV show called *Jersey Shore*. This was, to a person of Italian ancestry just about the worst depiction of the Italian people as you can get. The women were "loose," and the guys were "slobs." That's all I'm going to say about that. What I want to talk about is the incredible foods that mostly came from the Italian businesses and people living in the Garden State.

There were three distinct areas of Jersey and there were many foods that were unique to each area. Take North Jersey, for instance. As with New York City, North Jersey is renowned as the hot dog capital of the East. The most famous of these dogs was the "Ripper." Ask any native and they will have their own version of this delicious delicacy. The Ripper was a hot dog deep fried in oil until the casing bursts or "rips." They are served with spicy brown mustard, chopped onions, and a slab of chili on top.

The second most famous hot dog from North Jersey is my favorite, the Italian Hot Dog. This dog got its roots from a small restaurant named Jimmy Buff's in Newark in 1932. This hot dog is prepared using half a loaf of "Abbetz," a small, round, flat loaf of Italian bread with a small hole in the center. You slice this in half and dig out some of the middle bread, then line some of the interior with mustard. Two deep fried hot dogs are then stuffed into the pocket and topped with fried or sautéed onions and peppers and then on top of that goes deep fried or pan fried thinly sliced potatoes and a small smattering of ketchup.

Some diners use Italian sausages instead of hot dogs, but either way this makes for a filling and scrumptious lunch or dinner sandwich. You'll find these available on the "grease trucks" or lunch wagons that frequent the campuses of Rutgers University in New Brunswick. In addition, the grease trucks serve another concoction to students in need of multitudes of calories, and they are called "fat sandwiches." These things contain everything a hungry student could want; chicken fingers, mozzarella sticks, onion rings, and French fries all stuffed together inside a medium-sized hoagie roll.

Central Jersey is known for three very popular foods: a tomato pie, pork roll, and a sub. If you ask for a pizza you get the traditional pie with sauce over the dough and toppings on top of that. A "tomato pie" has the cheese on top of the dough, then the toppings, and finally the tomato sauce on top. This is a very tomato-intensive tasting pie and it has a pretty huge following.

Pork roll is a sausage-like pork meat product that was invented by a guy named John Taylor from Trenton back in the late nineteenth century. Pork roll is sold in a large, tube-like roll or sack and wrapped in plastic and then in a muslin sock over that. Some people call it Taylor ham or Taylor pork roll, not knowing the true origin of the product. Three-quarter inch slices are cut from the roll and placed in a hot fry pan or on a grill. After a couple of minutes, a knife is used to cut a line from the center out to the edge. As the pork roll is cooked, it shrivels and curls up and the slit helps keep it flat. Once it is grilled on one side, it is flipped and cooked on the other. It is served mainly on a Kaiser or "hard roll" with a fried egg, American cheese, and a splash of ketchup. If you have never tried it, I suggest that you give it a whirl; it's delicious.

Thirdly, the "sub." This is a sandwich that has many other names depending on where you grew up in the U.S. In the Northeast they are called grinders or heroes and other places call them po' boys or poor boys. But here in the good ol' Garden State we call them "subs," or submarine sandwiches. These are a medium loaf of French or Italian bread cut in half, layered with cold cuts (various meats and cheeses), and then drizzled with olive oil, vinegar, and some spices. They are generally served cold. No matter where you go in the entire state, you are bound to find a few dozen places that have at least five or six different types of subs on the menu. Try them!

Oh, I want to plug my favorite place to buy a sub, and that is Jersey Mike's Subs. They originated in Point Pleasant, New Jersey, and they're fast becoming a welcome sub joint all over the U.S.

Southern New Jersey is known for a few things, but nothing that is exclusively Italian: cranberries, blueberries, and saltwater taffy. Cranberries are grown in the bogs of South Jersey and blueberries are also harvested all over the southern end of the state. Saltwater taffy originated on the boardwalks of Atlantic City and has become as famous as the casinos that once flourished there.

Another not so well-known delicacy from the southern part of the state is a delicious, flavorful dish called the Panzoratti. Most people have heard of calzones, those small, folded over pizza dough sandwiches filled with mozzarella cheese and some pizza toppings. They are baked in an oven just like a pizza pie. Panzoratti follows the same idea, but it's deep fried instead and comes out with a deep golden-brown crust that tastes almost as sweet as a donut. Dip one into some warm marinara sauce and you have a pretty great tasting lunch or dinner.

On a final tribute to my home state, I must mention the New Jersey diner. The "diner" was first created by a guy named Jerry O' Mahoney who started a diner company in Elizabeth in 1912. Today there are over

525 diners still in operation in the state. These diners were originally thought to be replicas of the fancy railroad dining cars of the thirties and forties, but that wasn't the case. These restaurants never had wheels and were completely stationary. The big draw of the diner is that most of them are open 24/7 and they serve breakfast all day long. This of course is a big hit with the thousands of truckers who pass through the state north to south. Diners usually had four to six-seater booths and a jukebox that played mostly oldies from the fifties and sixties. Many also had motorized revolving dessert cases that would showcase their many homemade pies, cakes, puddings, and other tasty treats to tempt customers.

Most of the diners I went into growing up always served the usual hamburgers, hot dogs, milk shakes, and the previously mentioned pork roll sandwiches. But the thing I miss about the New Jersey diners was a place for friends and family to get together to chat, celebrate birthdays and other special occasions, and get some decent food without ever having to wash the dishes.

An elderly Italian man lay dying in his bed. While suffering the agonies of impending death, he suddenly smelled the aroma of his favorite Italian anisette pizzelle cookies wafting up the stairs from the kitchen. Gathering every bit of remaining strength, he lifted himself from his bed, leaned against the wall, and slowly made his way out of the bedroom to crawl downstairs. With gasping breaths, he leaned against the kitchen entryway peering onto the kitchen table where he noticed a large plate of freshly baked pizzelle cookies begging to be eaten.

His first thought was that his faithful wife of sixty years decided to make him one last final treat before leaving this world, and this would certainly make him happy. With one giant effort, he threw himself onto the table and reached out to grab a cookie. Just then a spatula came down and smacked his hand. Turning slightly, he saw and heard the growl of his devoted wife. "Get the hell outta here, you old fart. Those cookies are for the funeral."

FOCACCIA BREAD

3 cups all-purpose flour
1 package dry yeast
1 teaspoon sugar
3/4 cup warm water, between 105-115 degrees
1 teaspoon salt
1/3 cup olive oil

In a small bowl, pour about one-half cup of the warm water. Sprinkle the dry yeast on top of the water and let it set for about five minutes. Swirl the water once or twice to make sure it is all dissolved. A slight foam should form on top of the water. If it does not, the yeast is no good or the water was too hot.

In a large bowl, place the flour and add the salt to the flour. Make a hollow in the center of the flour and pour the yeast mixture into it along with the oil, sugar, and the rest of the water.

If you want to make an herb bread, add these spices now: 1-1/2 teaspoons of Italian seasoning or equal parts of sage, oregano, thyme, and ground rosemary to equal 1-1/2 teaspoons.

Another variation is just rosemary and sage together, about three-quarter teaspoon of each, ground well.

A third variation is to add some finely chopped onion along with finely chopped black or green olives and a couple teaspoons of finely grated parmesan cheese.

You can get creative here and add any combination of those items I mentioned and make your own variation.

With the add-ins mixed into the oil and yeast mixture, use a wooden spoon to gently mix in the flour until all the flour is incorporated. If the dough seems too dry, add more warm water; if it is too sticky, add more flour until it is nice and smooth and elastic. Turn the dough out onto a floured surface and begin to knead the dough. You must knead it constantly for seven to eight minutes to get it just right. Punch the dough, fold it over, then punch it again; keep doing this, smacking it against the table to develop the gluten. Place the ball of dough into a lightly greased bowl and cover it with a thick towel or cloth. Place the dough in a warm place, where it will need about one to two hours to rise.

After it rises, roll it out again on the floured surface. Knead it gently for a minute or two. You can roll the dough out with your hands or use a rolling pin. Roll it out to about the size of the baking pan you will be using. Make sure it has at least a two-inch high edge. Coat the pan lightly with oil and place the dough into the pan. Using your fingers, spread the dough out to all four edges. Poke dimples into the dough with your fingers. Cover the dough with a thick towel and let it rest for thirty minutes to a full hour. It will rise again slightly. If you want to add toppings, you can do it just before baking. Add tomato or onion slices, black or green olives, or even pepperoni slices. Chunks of raw garlic work well also. Be imaginative! Once the toppings are on the dough, pour some olive oil into your hands and rub it all over the dough. Bake in a Preheated 450-degree oven for about twenty-five minutes or until the edges are lightly browned. Baking time will depend on the thickness of the dough and the thickness of the baking pan, so watch it closely. This bread does not freeze well, so you will have to use it up within a couple of days. Better yet, give some to friends and let them marvel at your wonderful kitchen skills.

Let's take a moment to go back in time to your childhood. If you are approaching middle age, you will probably relate to many of the things that I remember as a kid. Some of you may not.

Here is a list of things I fondly remember:

Weekly Reader: This was a school handout newspaper that was written on a kid's level. I remember paying 10 cents a week to get the paper and I really loved the articles on space travel. It arrived every Wednesday and came rolled up with an elastic band around it, just like a real newspaper.

Silver Tinsel: Tinsel came in a long skinny box by Double-Glo. It was used to decorate the Christmas tree and some parents were very particular about putting it on the tree one strand at a time. This could sometimes take hours, but that tree sparkled like jewelry afterwards.

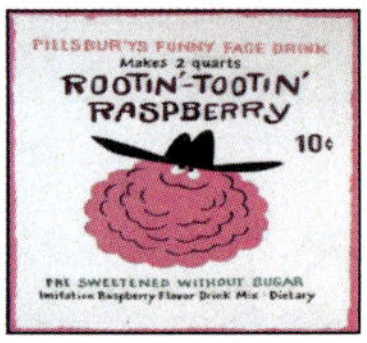

Rootin Tootin Raspberry Drink Mix: Pillsbury came out with these drink mixes to rival Kool-Aid. The packages had funny faces on them of fruits in funny disguises. My favorite was Goofy-Grape.

Kellogg's Jumbo Variety Cereal Pack: Kids couldn't get enough of these mini boxes of a variety of breakfast cereals. There were ten boxes in the package, but only about six different kinds of cereal. The best part of these was that the boxes could be cut with a knife, opened up like basement cellar doors, and you could pour milk right into the wax paper-lined interior of the box and eat it right there and then. It was perfect for camping or school trips.

Mattel's Thing Maker: This toy was on every kid's wish list. It was a kind of oven where you put a metal mold on the top, poured in some colored gel from a squeeze bottle, and then watched it bake into a bug or some other kind of creepy crawler. By far the best stuff to scare your little sisters with.

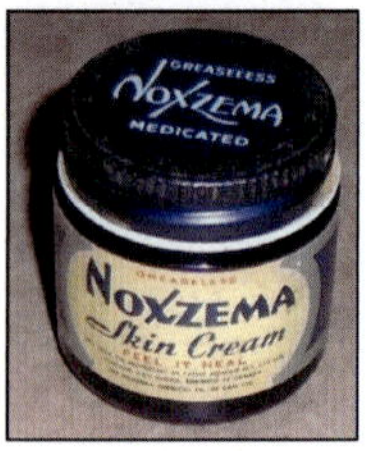

Noxzema Cream: Before sunscreen was invented, we had Noxzema. It came in a small cobalt blue jar and we kept it in the refrigerator—why, I don't know! It smelled like medicine, but when rubbed on, it cooled the skin like an ice cube.

Chef Boy-Ar-Dee: This company made mommy's work in the kitchen much easier. They made spaghetti in a can, corn beef hash, and an entire pizza in a box was even available. There were three packages: one was flour to mix with water then roll out, one was a plastic bag of some ketchup style sauce, and another contained some chemically manufactured grated cheese for the top. Yummy, you bet!

Bazooka Gum: As kids, we had our choice of many different kinds of gum, but most of us chose Bazooka. It was a huge wad of pink bubble gum that came wrapped in a comic strip. Since the comics were printed as a series, we used to trade our comic strips with other kids to finally get to read the whole story.

Life Savers Candy Christmas Book: One thing a kid could always count on for Christmas was getting a Life Savers Candy Christmas Book. It contained ten rolls of different kinds of Life Saver rolls of candies. I always traded my wintergreen roll for the butterscotch ones, but cherry was still my favorite.

Vaccines: Take a look at the bare shoulder of any adult over 60 years old and there might be a small, round circle with a bunch of dots in it. This is the scar that was left by the injection received for polio when he or she was a kid. I also remember getting another type of vaccination but this one was some kind of red medicine dropped onto a small cube of sugar. Doctors back then were smart; what kid would turn down eating a lump of sugar?

Evening in Paris: When you were young and didn't have a steady income, buying Christmas presents was tough to do. The good thing is that stores like Woolworth's and S.S. Kreske sold a cologne that every mother wanted, and it was cheap. For $2.25 a kid could surprise his mom at Christmas with a bottle of Evening in Paris. That 3-ounce cobalt blue bottle of cologne with the silver cap and a small silver ribbon tied around the neck was so strong that a single bottle would last her at least eight years.

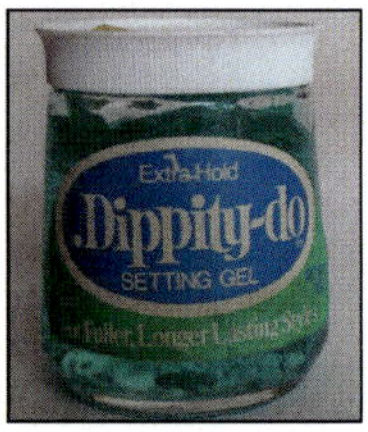

Dippity-Do: If you had as many sisters as I did growing up, there were probably at least two jars of this stuff called Dippity-Do lying around. As sisters often would, before going out on a date, they would put their hair up in curlers and dab some of this styling gel on it to make it set. Once removing the curlers, the hair would be curly and cute (I guess). I tried using it as a substitute for model airplane glue when I ran out, but it didn't work as well.

Farber Erasers: When I first started learning how to type on a typewriter, I wasn't very good. I made lots of mistakes. I had this really nifty eraser that looked like a giant white wheel the size of a silver dollar and it had a small brush on it. It came in handy for erasing my many mistakes on my old Smith-Corona typewriter.

Well, I hope you enjoyed this little trip down memory lane. It was fun for me to reminisce, too.

I accidentally stole twenty-six half-gallons of milk from a milk machine when I was a kid. When I say "accidentally," I really mean it. Mom gave me a quarter and asked me to walk up to the corner gas station and get a quart of milk out of a milk vending machine they used to have there. Machines like this were seen all over, but mostly outside convenience stores and gas stations. They were convenient because if the store was closed, you could still buy milk. This particular machine was owned and maintained by Krauzer's Dairy. Anyway, I put the quarter in the slot as I had done many times before and selected a quart of regular whole milk. The machine did nothing. Usually it would start making this

humming noise, and then some mechanical device would dispense the selected product down a shoot. This time, nothing happened. I reached up for the coin return lever and pressed it a few times. Out came two quarters. I was astonished. Naturally, I pocketed the second quarter and inserted the first one; again, still nothing. Back to the coin return lever. This time, NOTHING! So, being the faithful son that I was, I reached into my pocket and took out the other quarter and inserted it into the coin slot and selected the quart button. Again, nothing happened. I was kind of frustrated by now, so I frantically started pushing every button on the machine. Suddenly it came to life and started making this whirling noise and out popped a half-gallon of milk. I opened the door, retrieved the milk and turned to go home. As I started walking away, the machine woke up again and started making that whirring noise and once again a half-gallon of milk appeared in the delivery shoot. "Whoa," I commented to myself. Two half-gallons of milk for 50 cents. As I reached in to grab the second container, one more appeared after that and one more again and it finally stopped at 26. I panicked. I wasn't sure what to do, so I took all the half-gallons and hid them in the thick grass behind the machine. I ran home to get my Radio Flyer wagon and high-tailed it back to the defective machine. I put all the milk in my wagon and started for home.

As I approached the intersection of Mason Drive and Willowbrook, I took notice of a red light flashing atop a police car that was racing down the street towards me. I turned around and there was another police car behind me. Soon enough there were three cars with lights flashing and they had me surrounded. My heart was beating so fast I thought I was going to faint. Here I was in the middle of the road with three cop cars, opened doors, lights flashing, CB radios blasting away some garbled noise, and me—holding on to the handle of my wagon for dear life. "Where'd ya get all that milk young feller?" the cop asked.

As I opened my mouth to try and explain, another cop chimed in and shouted, "Mrs. Taylor saw you stealing it, so don't deny it!" The third cop didn't say a word; he just opened the trunk of the cop car and started putting in all the milk. "Come on," he finally said. "We're taking you for a little ride." I got into the police car and we sped off down Middle Road to the police station. Once at the station, a sergeant started asking me questions and then they let me call my mother. Since my mother didn't drive, she ran over to our neighbor's house and asked if she could get a lift to the station.

Mom wound up paying $50 to a county clerk to let me go, but I did have to appear in court the following Friday. Long story short, I explained everything to the judge, and they let me go, gave us the milk to keep, and I got off with just a reprimand. The judge said that I should have called Krauzer's Dairy from the gas station and let them handle it. I guess I could have, but that darn machine ate up my only quarter from the very beginning. We froze all the milk and used it up within the next couple of months. We made lots of homemade chocolate pudding, which is my favorite, especially using fresh, whole milk. I'll share my recipe for this delicious and easy to make pudding.

CHOCOLATE OR VANILLA PUDDING

1/3 cup Hershey's Dark Unsweetened Cocoa

2/3 cup sugar

3 heaping tablespoons corn starch

2 teaspoons vanilla extract

2 pats of butter

2 cups whole milk

Pinch of salt

For vanilla pudding you will need 1 beaten egg yolk.

Mix the cocoa with the sugar and corn starch and a pinch of salt.

Place into a medium-sized sauce pan and pour in the milk. Begin using medium heat and stir the mixture constantly until it starts to boil and get thick. Continue cooking for about two minutes more, still stirring. Remove from heat and add the vanilla and the butter. Stir until it is combined. Immediately place a piece of plastic wrap directly over the hot pudding to prevent a skin from forming. Cool before using.

Use the same recipe for vanilla except eliminate the cocoa and add the beaten egg yolk to the milk mixture. Makes about 4 servings.

Here are a few ideas on what to do with those wonderful puddings you just made.

Chocolate Pudding Pie

Chocolate Pudding

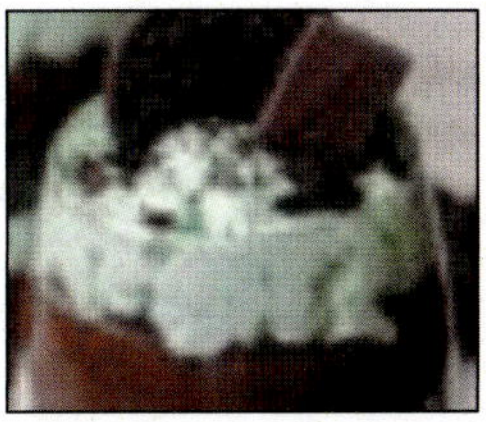

Chocolate Mint Dessert

Dirt Cups

Line an 8-inch glass or metal pie pan with a store-brought pie crust. Prick holes all around with a fork and bake in a 350-degree oven for about fifteen minutes or until golden brown. You can use a second pie pan on top of this one for the first eight or so minutes so that bubbles don't develop in the crust. Fill the pan with some rice and then bake. Cool completely and fill with chocolate or vanilla pudding. Cool and cover with Cool Whip or fresh whipped cream. You can also use only vanilla pudding; substitute the vanilla extract for banana-flavored extract. Let the pudding cool and then bake a crust as described above, cool it, and line with sliced bananas and pour the pudding in. Let cool and cover with whipped cream for a delicious banana cream pie.

Pre-made graham cracker dessert tart cups can be filled with chocolate pudding, then heat up some raspberry preserves in a microwave for just a minute, pour a small amount over the cooled pudding, and top with a fresh raspberry or two and a sprig of mint. This makes a nice light dessert to enjoy after a hearty pasta or lasagna dinner.

You could also make chocolate mint parfait desserts. Layer chocolate pudding in a glass. Flavor Cool Whip topping with a drop of mint extract and a drop of green food coloring. Crush up some chocolate cream cookies and make two more layers. Top with more cookie crumbs, another sandwich cookie, and mint flavored after-dinner chocolate candies.

Dirt cups are a kid's favorite. Add some chocolate syrup to cool whip, layer chocolate pudding and cool whip with crushed chocolate sandwich cookie crumbs. Top with more crumbs and gummy worms. These are also quick ways to make favorite birthday treats.

Lastly, you can whip up a nice refrigerator cake. Make two batches of pudding. One vanilla and one chocolate. Layer graham crackers or vanilla wafers into a 9"x9" square glass baking dish. Spread alternate layers of either pudding on top of the crackers and make three layers. Top with graham crackers and cover with plastic wrap. Refrigerate overnight.

Spread the top with whipped topping or cool whip and cut into squares just before serving.

Jim and I snapped this photo of us while in Cinque Terre on the northwest coast of Italy, known as Liguria. It was published in the Travel Section of the Sunday edition of the *Denver Post*, along with a short story of our visit to the "Five Lands". If you ever get the chance to visit Italy, don't pass up this part of the country. There are five amazing towns all connected by the local train and each town has its own station. Above the villages are trails that link together to make up a national park. There is a fee to hike through them, but it's certainly worth doing. I highly recommend sitting down and enjoying one of the local wines. They will be mostly whites and they are on the slightly sweet side. You cannot get any fresher fish than in Cinque Terre because the local fishermen catch and sell each day to the local restaurants. Oh, and watch out for the stray cats; there are lots of them around town.

Here is another of those five-minute recipes I promised. Well, it may be a bit more than five minutes, but it is definitely not labor-intensive.

SHRIMP SCAMPI

2 tablespoons olive oil
2 pats of butter
1/4 cup lemon juice
3 tablespoons shallots, finely minced
3 medium garlic cloves, minced
2 lbs. medium to jumbo shrimp, deveined

Combine the olive oil and the butter with the lemon juice, then add the minced shallots and garlic. Spread this on the bottom of a glass baking dish. Rinse and dry the shrimp. Drop them into the baking dish and coat them with the oil mixture on both sides. Turn on the broiler just before preparing to serve dinner and place the dish under the broiler. Cook the shrimp for about two minutes, then turn them over and cook for another one minute.

I like to serve this over angel hair pasta, which takes only a few minutes to cook. Spritz the shrimp with a bit more lemon juice and sprinkle dried parsley over the pasta and shrimp for presentation. Don't forget the garlic bread and a glass of white zinfandel to accompany this wonderful meal. Serves 4-6 people.

Kitchen Tip: To prevent you from crying up a storm when cutting an onion, peel the skin and place the whole onion in the freezer for about 20 minutes. You can now dice or mince with a dry eye in the house.

For a couple of summers, our family had a time share at "The Shore." If you're from New Jersey, you don't say "the beach." You say "the shore." My Aunt Kay and her family and ours shared a rental for two weeks of the summer at Wildwood Crest way down to almost the end of New Jersey. It was a very small, bungalow-type beach house about a quarter mile from the water. The boardwalk in Wildwood had lots of amusement rides on a couple of piers, and it was always a treat to get to go and spend the week while on vacation. The thing was, we all couldn't go at once; there were just too many kids, and not enough room in the station wagon for all the kids, plus beach stuff, food, pots and pans, and towels. So only four kids got to go. We naturally used the democratic way of deciding who should go and who should stay. We drew straws. I was one of the lucky ones one year and got to stay the whole week. I managed to save up about $3 to spend on rides and to buy stuff on the boardwalk at night.

We chose Wildwood as our getaway mainly because it was the most decent and farthest beach from New York City. See, in the summertime all the "bennies," as we called them—that is, people from the city, would flock to every available New Jersey beach area, leaving their suburban hot boxes and smelly concrete high rises to mingle with the Jerseyites. Most of the New Yorkers were too lazy to drive clear down to the end of New Jersey which is where Wildwood was.

Wildwood was the only "free" beach back then on the entire Jersey Shore. Buying each of the kid's beach badges was a small hunk of change so mom was sure glad we chose a free beach.

When you're a kid raising hell in the vacation wonderland of New Jersey, no one cared what kind of food you ate. After all, you're on the beach, it's summer, and anything goes. While the boardwalk concession stands sold everything from hoagies, to pizza, to clams on a half shell, alongside sausage and pepper sandwiches and calzones, we kids were reminded that mom packed along lots of cold eggplant parmesan sandwiches and iced tea. So, this was my life for a whole week, eggplant for lunch, pizza for dinner, and sun and surf every day. Life, when you were seven, was good. So, if it is summer and if you only have an hour or so to get dinner on the table, try this quick recipe.

STUFFED CHICKEN BREAST FLORENTINE

6 small-to-medium skinless chicken breasts, trimmed of all fat

15-oz. container of ricotta cheese

10-oz. package of frozen spinach, thawed and well drained

2 eggs, beaten

8-oz. package of shredded mozzarella cheese

1 jar of cheap spaghetti sauce, marinara or basil and tomato

Salt and pepper

1 tablespoon finely chopped garlic

1 handful of Pinoli nuts, chopped, if you have them

Butterfly the chicken breasts (slice them along the long side to within an inch of the edge but not completely through).

Open them up and season both sides with salt and pepper.

In a medium bowl, combine the ricotta cheese, eggs, spinach, garlic, about three-quarters of the mozzarella cheese and the pine nuts, if you have them.

Stuff each of the chicken breasts with the ricotta mix, divided evenly.

Push a few long toothpicks into the breasts to hold them together. Layer some tomato sauce in the bottom of a baking pan. Lay the breasts in the pan and cover with the remainder of the tomato sauce. Make sure to cover all of the exposed chicken. Top each with the remaining mozzarella cheese, then bake in a preheated 350-degree oven for about one hour. Check with a small knife for no pink remaining, but don't over bake them. Good side dishes are mashed potatoes and green beans. This serves six people.

When I was in the seventh grade, I was bused to yet another middle school. This school was in a very affluent area of central New Jersey called Colt's Neck. The kids were snobby, the neighborhood was full of yuppies and giant houses, and the rich kids always teased the poor kids. Needless to say, I felt so out of place there.

The only saving grace to going to Colt's Neck Elementary was that on the way home, the bus driver stopped to get a coffee at a little coffee shop type café known to every kid in that neighborhood as "Tiny Glenn's." The reason it was called Tiny Glenn's was because it was owned by two little people named Glen and Glenn. These guys were not much fun to talk to, but they had a good sense of humor and didn't let their size get in the way of them running that luncheonette. At 13 years old, I was constantly hungry and getting a plate of take out Mac and cheese to eat on the way home wasn't going to spoil my dinner.

The food served by these little guys was incredible, but I especially loved their 25-cent plate of mac and cheese. It was creamy, cheesy, and had toasted breadcrumbs on top. I never got the recipe, but I recreated a close variation of it by trial and error. I think my version is just as good as Glenn's.

MAC AND CHEESE

2 cups cooked elbow macaroni (reserve some of the cooking water)

1/2 cup butter, divided

1/8 cup flour

3 cups whole milk

1 cup shredded mild cheddar cheese

1 cup shredded Colby Jack cheese

1 cup processed cheese (Velveeta) or 6 slices yellow American cheese

1/2 cup mozzarella cheese, shredded

2/3 cup breadcrumbs

1 large tomato, cut in thin slices

Salt and pepper

Cook the elbow macaroni al dente. Combine all the shredded cheeses and cut the American cheese into small pieces. Melt one quarter cup of butter and add the flour while stirring constantly. Add the milk gradually and continue to stir. Cook on medium heat just until tiny bubbles form on the milk. Add all the cheeses and melt everything. Add a pinch of salt and about one-eighth teaspoon of black pepper, more or less, to taste.

Pour a small amount of the cheese in the bottom of a large glass baking pan. Add some of the cooked macaroni. Add a bit of water to the remaining cheese sauce so that it is very pourable. Place the sliced tomatoes on top of the macaroni and pour the remaining cheese over the rest of the elbows. Bake in a 350-degree oven for about thirty-five minutes, or until the top layer of cheese is nice and brown and bubbly. In a small saucepan, melt the remaining butter and add the breadcrumbs. Cook for a minute or two or until they become nice and browned. Sprinkle over the mac and cheese and bake for an additional five or so minutes.

This is another topping that goes well with the mac and cheese: open a can of stewed tomatoes and heat them in a saucepan. Open a can of white albacore tuna fish and break up the tuna then add it to the stewed tomatoes. Heat to almost boiling. Upon serving the mac and cheese, pour on some of the tuna/tomato mixture. Try this—you'll love it. It not only adds flavor, but it makes mac and cheese almost a completely nutritious meal. Serves 6.

FAMILY SHARE: SISTER KATHY SERIO

The year was 1967. We were newlyweds living in a three-room apartment in Carteret, New Jersey. My husband, Frank, was a creature of habit and would come from work weekdays at exactly 5 pm. His routine was to shower, shave, walk the dog, and read the paper in that order. After dinner, he would sit and watch the television from around 8 pm to 11:30 pm. He preferred to watch in "peace and quiet." He was generally a social guy, but when 8 pm rolled around, he didn't want to be bothered by talking to anyone; he just wanted to watch his shows.

One evening, my baby sister Maryann, who was just 11 years old at the time, was sleeping over. She and Frank used to joke around all the time, and she knew most of his peculiar ways. This particular night, we were trying to get Frank away from his "shows" and into a meaningful conversation. I suggested she mention something about the U.S. Navy. Frank had served for over two years and he loved talking about it to anyone who would listen.

Maryann asked him about the military alphabet, and then started reciting the code ... Alpha, Beta, Ceta, Deta... She and I started laughing so hard because he got so mad and thought we were making fun of it. She really wasn't though. She just didn't know the right sequence was Alpha, Beta, Charlie, Delta, etc., and neither did I. The more we laughed, the madder he became. Finally, he got up, gave a couple of hand gestures, and went to bed. Before doing so, he snatched the TV cord off the back of the set and took it with him "for spite." Maryann felt so badly afterwards that he had gotten so upset and missed his precious TV shows. I told her that since a way to a man's heart is through his stomach, she should make his lunch for him and put an apology note in it. So, she did.

The next day when Frank came home from work, he was fuming. He kept saying that he was never so humiliated in his whole life. Everyone at work was laughing at him when he bit into his sandwich and came up with the soggy piece of paper—the apology note.

Of course, I started laughing again and couldn't stop just thinking of how funny that must have been biting into a ham and cheese and paper sandwich. After I calmed down, I explained that "she was just an 11-year-old." It took him a while, but he finally forgave her for the embarrassment.

Frank has passed on now, but to this day, anytime I mention Alpha, Beta, Ceta, and Deta, my sisters will all recall that incident, and we all would again begin to laugh out loud.

STUFFED PEPPERS

4 green, red, orange, or yellow peppers (mix them for color)

3 mild or hot Italian sausage links or 6 oz. ground sausage meat

1 lb. ground beef

8 oz. fresh spinach leaves

1 teaspoon each of salt, pepper, and onion powder

1 tablespoon fresh parsley

1 egg

1 cup cooked risotto

1/2 jar of marinara sauce, about 8 oz. (use canned tomato sauce in a pinch)

1/4 cup grated parmesan cheese

Mix the meats together along with the egg and spices. Brown the meats with a little olive oil until no pink remains. Drain the fat from the pan. Add the cooked rice and spinach leaves and stir until combined. Add about five ounces of tomato sauce. Place the cleaned and cored peppers in a foil-lined baking dish and stuff them with the ground beef mixture. Place a tablespoon of the remaining tomato sauce over each one. Cover the peppers with aluminum foil and bake in a 350-degree oven for approximately thirty-five minutes. One option is to place a slice of mozzarella or American yellow cheese over each and let them bake for an additional five minutes, or until the cheese is melted.

I also like adding some breadcrumbs over the meat before the sauce to add some crunchiness to the peppers. These are best when served directly from the oven. Serves 4.

If you are like me, and you enjoy having dinner guests over for a light meal and cards or games, there is nothing more stressful than making a dinner that keeps you cooped up in the kitchen for hours. I recently had one such event. Since I thought of everything way in advance, it was really easy to throw everything together once guests arrived, and I was able to sit and entertain along with my friends. My menu consisted of mini shepherds' pies, a tossed salad, and for dessert a delicious Italian cream cake. I started a week ahead and made the cake. This cake freezes well and defrosts within two hours. I'll get to the other recipes in a bit.

ITALIAN CREAM CAKE

For the Cake:

1 stick of salted butter, softened
1/2 cup Crisco shortening
2 cups sugar
5 egg yolks
1 cup buttermilk
(whole milk with 2-3 teaspoons of lemon juice as a substitute)
1 teaspoon vanilla extract
1 teaspoon baking soda
2 cups flour
1/2 cup shredded coconut
1 cup chopped pecans
5 beaten egg whites

For the Frosting:

1 stick unsalted butter softened

1 package low fat or regular cream cheese, softened

1 teaspoon vanilla extract

1 box or more of confectioners' sugar

1/2 cup chopped pecans

1/2 cup shredded coconut

Preheat the oven to 325 degrees. Spray or grease a 9x13 baking dish with Crisco or cooking spray.

In a large bowl or stand mixer bowl, mix the butter together with the shortening and sugar and beat until smooth. Add the egg yolks one at a time and blend each one. In another small bowl, mix the buttermilk with the vanilla extract and the baking soda.

Add a little flour mixture to the butter mixture and add some liquid. Continue this alternating with each one until all mixed in.

Beat the egg whites until stiff.

Add the pecans, coconut, and egg whites into the batter and fold in until all is incorporated. Pour into the greased pan.

Bake for about forty minutes and then lower the heat to 225 degrees. Continue baking for an additional ten or so minutes, or until a toothpick inserted in the center comes out clean.

Remove from oven and let cool completely. Chill in refrigerator.

Make a frosting using one stick of softened butter and an eight-ounce package of softened cream cheese. Add a teaspoon of vanilla extract. Mix together in a bowl and add confectioners' sugar until it reaches a nice, smooth consistency.

Place some shredded coconut under a broiler and lightly toast until a golden brown. Try a toaster oven for this as well. Watch carefully as it only takes a few minutes to burn coconut.

Once the cake is nice and chilled, frost the cake and then garnish with toasted coconut and pecan pieces.

Now cover with aluminum foil or plastic wrap and put it in the freezer until the day of the gathering.

MINI SHEPHERD'S PIES

- 2 packages refrigerated pie crusts
- 1 tablespoon olive oil
- 2-3 tablespoons all-purpose flour
- 1 large onion, chopped
- 2 large or 3 medium carrots, peeled and chopped fine
- 2 large or 3 medium garlic cloves, chopped
- 1 cup frozen corn
- 1 cup frozen peas
- 1 lb. ground beef
- 2-3 tablespoons butter
- Fresh parsley, chopped
- 1 cup low-sodium beef broth (or brown gravy seasoning and water to equal one cup)
- 1-2 cups prepared mashed potatoes

You can prepare these crusts ahead of time and freeze them. Roll out two to three sheets of refrigerated pie crust dough on a lightly floured surface. For smaller pies, use a regular 2.5-inch muffin tin. Using a 3.5-inch drink glass, press out as many three-and-a-half sized circles as you can get from the pie crust. Grease the muffin tins and line each with a round of pie crust dough. Press evenly around the sides and bottom. For larger pies, use a 3.5-inch muffin tin and a glass or bowl that measures around five-and-a-half inches. The recipe to follow will make six large or twelve small pies.

Bake the crusts in a 375-degree oven until lightly browned. After a few minutes check them and if they are getting bubbles, push the crusts back against the bottom and sides using a cork or a shot glass then continue baking. Once baked, let them cool and remove from muffin tins. Place them in an aluminum pan and cover with plastic wrap and freeze them if doing this ahead of time.

If you are making these pies on the same day, continue on to make the filling.

For the filling:

In a large skillet, heat the oil and add the onion, carrots, and garlic. Cook for about ten minutes or until the carrots are softened. Add the ground beef and continue to cook until no pink is showing. Drain the juices from the pan. Stir in the frozen peas and corn. Move the beef mixture to one side and melt the butter in the pan. Add some flour and alternate with some liquid broth using a whisk to make a gravy. Once thickened, combine with the meat mixture and cook for a few minutes covered. The mixture should be pretty thick.

Fill the freshly baked or baked and defrosted pie shells to within a quarter inch from the top. Layer some mashed potatoes on each one and place them under a broiler to brown the tops of the potatoes. Garnish with some fresh parsley before serving.

TOSSED SALAD WITH WALNUTS & RASPBERRY VINAIGRETTE

2 heads romaine lettuce, shredded

2 small peeled and cored gala apples, cut into small chunks or slices

4 oz. dried cranberries

4 oz. crushed walnut pieces

1 8-oz. container of fresh raspberries

For the Dressing:

2 oz. olive oil

2 teaspoons raspberry jam, with or without seeds

3 tablespoons walnut oil

2 teaspoons tarragon leaves

Pinch of salt and pepper

1 teaspoon honey mustard

Place the salad fixings except the raspberries in a medium sized bowl. Combine all the dressing ingredients together in a small jar with a lid and mix vigorously. Cut the raspberries into pieces and place on salad. Add dressing to taste.

When we were just kids my brothers and I would wander off aimlessly, exploring not only our neighborhood, but as we got braver, more distant ones. One particular Sunday evening in late October, we ventured into a cemetery. We didn't know what it was by its entrance since there were no signs, markings or pillars—just a rusty old gate and overgrown hedges. We stumbled across some gravestones, also overgrown and unkempt. Some were knocked down, and many were just naturally falling over on their own. It was an eerie place to be sure, but what made it even more frightening was that as the sun started to set, and as the last faint glimpses of sunlight disappeared, a mysterious green glow bathed the tombstones. As we walked deeper into the wooded area, the green haze became more intense. Looking up into the night sky, there was no source for the light. There were no telephone poles from which to hang a light. There were no buildings with windows to shed any kind of light. It was just as strange as could be. The later it got, the more scared we became. Finally, my brothers pleaded with me to get them the heck out of there. Good thing my Scout training helped me to remember the trail and we headed straight for the exit.

The next day at school, I told my friend John about my experience. He said that we must have been in "Greenlight Cemetery." I asked him how he knew of it, and he told me that he and a couple of friends also ventured into the place and discovered the eeriness of the green light. I asked him if he knew where the green light came from, and he admitted that they never found its source either. I told John that we would have to go there another time in the daylight, so we could find out where that light was coming from, and we agreed.

We were all of about 16, but John was 17 and he knew how to drive. His dad gave him this old 1958 Buick Regal station wagon to scoot around in. It weighed about four tons and out of the eight original cylinders, only four were still working.

Some school mornings, when the bus was late, John would pull up and shuffle us to school in the "death wagon," which is what we called it. It would huff and puff and sputter along about three miles per hour, sucking about a gallon of gas for every mile it went.

About two weeks later, on a rather cold and rainy afternoon, John pulled up with the death wagon and a bunch of us got in and proceeded to the Greenlight Cemetery. As we drove through the gate, the Buick ran over a large downed tree trunk and got stuck. The wheels started spinning but the car was so heavy it only dug itself more deeply into the mud. My brothers and I got out and went around to the back of the car. We started heaving the car back and forth while John pushed the Drive and Reverse buttons on the dashboard. The car yanked forward a bit then backwards a bit and after many tries, John floored the gas pedal and the beast lunged forward; it only stopped after running over the entire Smock family graves—all five of them. We rushed over to the car and John got out to survey the damage. We all were in disbelief and then stood there laughing over the whole incident. John suggested that we get the car out of there because by now it had started raining even harder, and he was afraid the car would sink into a grave of its own.

No one we knew ever ventured out into that cemetery ever again, and we never did find out about the green light. Eventually we lost interest in the mystery surrounding Greenlight Cemetery.

FAMILY SHARE: COUSIN DIANE DEWLAND

When I was a little girl, around 10 years old, I went to visit my grandparents who lived in upstate New York. As the grownups sat around the kitchen table one evening, my grandmother went over to a stool that was next to the fridge. On that stool was a large tin can, covered with contact paper. Gram pulled off the lid and grabbed a handful of "frappe" cookies, placed them in a dish, and set them on the table. I had never seen these before, but since everyone was reaching for them, I did also. These deep-fried, sweet dough cookies covered in powdered sugar were the best thing I ever tasted. I reached for a second one and was told that one was plenty. Well, for me, one wasn't plenty. I had to find a way to get more. Once everyone had gone to bed, I snuck downstairs, careful to not step on the couple of stair treads that squeaked and found my way to that tin can in the kitchen. Here I was in my footed PJs, sitting on the floor scarfing down as many of those wonderful crispy cookies as my tummy could hold. After that I went back upstairs to bed.

The next morning, I awoke to the smell of breakfast and rushed down to the kitchen. I took my seat and said my good mornings to everyone. Suddenly everyone stopped what they were doing and started laughing. Now, I was red in the face, wondering what all the fuss was about. Someone finally pointed to my cute, chubby round face and pointed out the large ring of powdered sugar that covered it. I remember crawling under the table at that point. Aside from the embarrassment, I will never forget the taste of those wonderful cookies.

The following recipe was one that my dad, Leonard Ricci, Sr., used in his restaurant.

MY DAD'S FRAPPE RECIPE

For this recipe, I don't use a bowl mainly because it is much easier and fun to make it right on the kitchen or dining room table.

Place four cups of all-purpose flour in a circle on the table. Make a well in the center about twelve inches wide. Crack then drop four large eggs in the well and add two to three tablespoons of softened butter to the eggs. Mix the butter into the eggs until well combined. Add a pinch of salt, a half-teaspoon of baking powder, and about a quarter cup of Grand Marnier to the egg mixture. If you don't have Grand Marnier, use anise extract (1 teaspoon) or some other orange-flavored extract.

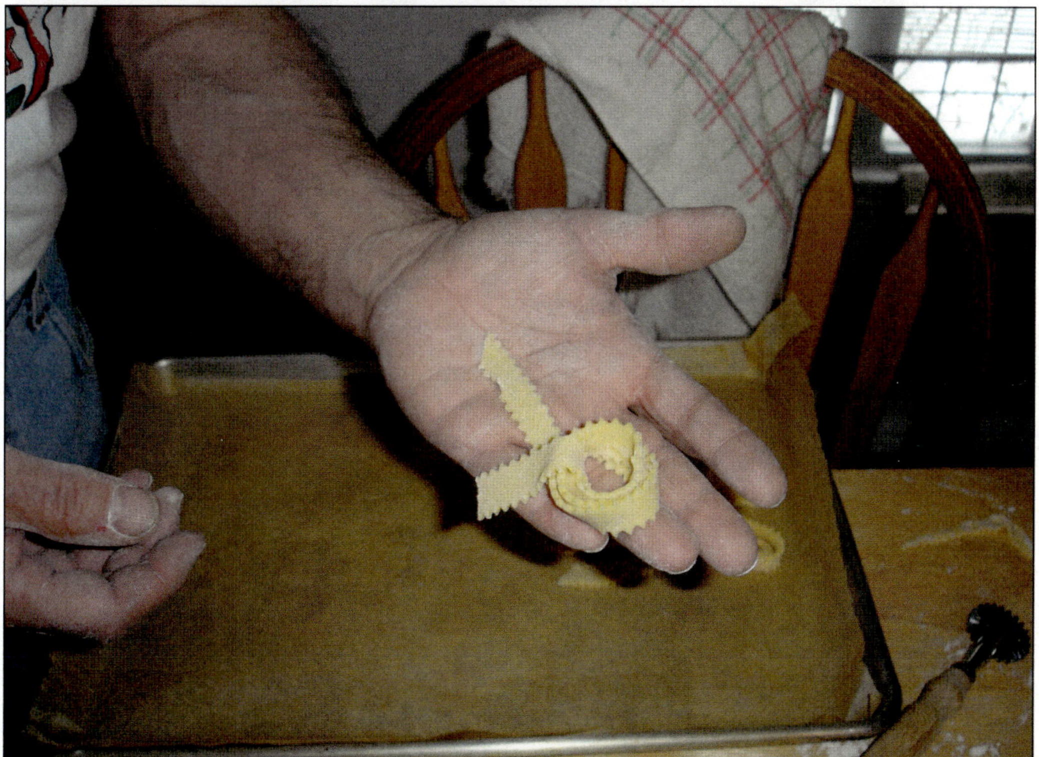

Begin to pull some flour into the center and mix it with the eggs. Continue adding small amounts of flour until a nice smooth dough forms. Continue kneading the dough. Once it is smooth and elastic, but not sticky, take and place the dough in a glass bowl. Clean off the table and if there is some flour left over, sprinkle it over the clean surface. Cut off half of the dough and cover the remainder with plastic wrap or a dish towel so it doesn't dry out. Roll the dough out with a rolling pin to about one-eighth inch thickness. Using a jagged edge pizza cutter, start at the center of the dough and cut strips of dough roughly one to 1-1/2 inches wide and about fourteen inches long. Using three fingers of the left hand, wrap the strip of dough around them about three times and insert the small, loose end through the center to make a bow tie. Make sure to leave a small tail on the end (see photo) of the strip and lay the cookies on a sheet of waxed paper. They should look like wreaths with two tails on them. Continue cutting out strips going towards the outer edge. When left with nothing but the smaller pieces, just squash them all together and re-roll the dough. The prepared cookies should dry about thirty minutes before frying.

Place about three inches of vegetable oil in a large, deep fry pan. Test the oil for readiness by dropping a piece of dough into it. It should sink and immediately rise to the top then start to bubble all around. Drop three or four cookies in at one time and cook until they reach a light brown; be careful because they cook very quickly. Once slightly browned on one side, flip them over. Remove them from the oil and set them on paper towels or brown paper to dry. These are best served warm and sprinkled with powdered sugar. If the plan is to store them, don't sugar them until you serve them. Taking after my cousin Diane, I suggest a large potato chip or pretzel tin with a nice tight lid. The cookies will stay fresh for a good three weeks—if they last that long, that is.

Saturday mornings around our house were kind of hectic, as one can well imagine. With that many kids running around, breakfast was total chaos. The frying pan was filled with scrambled eggs, the coffee pot was percolating, and the old two-slice toaster didn't stop once until the entire loaf of Wonder Bread was used up. Kid after kid would come down for breakfast, grab a plate, dish out some eggs and oatmeal, toast and orange juice, and scarf it all down within minutes, barely stopping to breathe between bites. If one of us was late for breakfast, it might mean last night's cold pasta fagioli.

I managed to get in on the second shift and dished myself out the last scrapings of the scrambled eggs. I grabbed the last two pieces of bread from the Wonder Bread bag and snickered. "How come nobody eats the ends"? I hated the end pieces too, but if that's all there is, I couldn't complain too much. I popped them into the toaster and sat there patiently waiting…and waiting. Finally, I realized that those tiny little wires weren't lighting up red like they should. I shook the toaster, pushed the lever up and down a few times, and still—nothing. Darn!

"Mom," I yelled, "someone broke the toaster!" Mom chimed back. "Well, there isn't much I can do about that now. I have to get the laundry started or you kids will be wearing last week's underwear all over again."

After the morning rush was over, I decided to "tinker" with the toaster. I discovered that one of the tiny heating wires was broken and this toaster had seen its last slice of bread.

I pulled out the Sears catalog and flipped through the pages of small appliances. I searched for the toasters and found one that sold for $12. "If we all pooled our money together, we could get a new one from Sears," I said. Mom replied, "I have a better idea. Go grab as many kids as you can find and gather around the dining room table."

"Okay," I said and rushed off into the back yard. I rounded up my two brothers and four sisters and we all marched into the dining room and sat down. Mom came in with a huge plastic cookie tin and plopped it on the table. She started pulling out stamps. S&H green stamps, plaid Stamps, blue stamps, and gold stamps. Then she gave each one of us a book. "Everyone take a book and start licking," she demanded. "I'm sure we have enough stamps to get two toasters."

Back in the late fifties and throughout the sixties, every grocery store, gas station, and even some department stores gave out "free" stamps when you purchased food and gas. Mom saved every single stamp she could get her hands on. She even traded with some neighbors' green ones for plaid ones, since the green ones were worth more.

For the next hour or so, we licked, and licked, and pasted, and pasted some more. We eventually filled up thirteen green stamp books, eight plaid stamp books, and three blue stamp books.

Later that week, we took a ride to the Green Stamp Redemption Center where we picked out a beautiful, brand new, *four*-slice toaster. And it only cost us eleven filled books of stamps.

Americans are in love with pizza which hails from Naples, Italy, as well as with pesto, which came from Genoa and, of course, biscotti which originated in Tuscany. The poor tortellini doesn't get mentioned too often in many cookbooks. The peasants of Liguria created these little morsels of heaven and everyone has improved them in some way or another. These days they come stuffed with shrimp, crab, beef, pork, and even prosciutto ham. The recipe that follows is just plain cheese tortellini with a delicious walnut sauce. Try it as an appetizer or even a light main dish, all for under a half hour of prep.

TORTELLINI WITH WALNUT SAUCE

1 lb. cheese-filled tortellini
1-1/2 cups walnut pieces
1 cup fresh basil leaves
1/2 cup fresh parsley
1 small garlic clove, minced
1 15-oz. container of whole milk ricotta cheese
1 teaspoon salt
1/2 teaspoon black pepper
Grated parmesan cheese

Cook the pasta as directed and drain, reserving about a half-cup of the hot water.

In a food processor, puree the walnut pieces, basil, parsley, and garlic. Add the ricotta cheese and the spices. Add the hot water a little at a time to make a thick but pourable sauce. Toss with warm pasta and serve with grated cheese, garlic bread, and of course a nice hearty burgundy or chianti wine. Now, wasn't that easy? Recipe makes about 4 servings.

As like every Saturday morning for weeks, this one started off with me counting my money. I pulled open the sock drawer and dragged out my sister Celia's old eyeglass case from the back. I hid my money in there because my brothers would never think to look there—if ever—should they plan on robbing me, which was often. It was $17 and some change. Just another $10, I thought, as I conjured up the vision of my new three-speed red Schwinn bicycle standing in the front window of W.T. Grant's department store. Down the stairs I sped, practically running into my mother at the kitchen sink. Anxiously trying to get her attention, I blurted out, "Mom, is there anything I can do today to make $10?"

"Not really," she replied, "but I do have a thought. Mrs. Hedaway up on High View Circle has an attic that needs cleaning. I was talking to her on the phone the other day and she asked if one of you boys could take care of that."

"You didn't tell Pat or Richard about this, did you"? I asked hopefully.

"No," she said. "I didn't get a chance to."

"Good," I said. "I'll do it." And with that, I ran out of the house and up to Mrs. Hedaway's. I was out of breath as I started knocking like a madman. She finally came to the door and I said I was there to clean out her attic. "Great! Let's go have a look, shall we?" she said enthusiastically.

As we opened the attic door, I knew that there were at least five hours worth of work here, so with my quick figuring I came up with my price: "Ten dollars and 25 cents," I said. She said that would be fine, but that I must do a complete job, and that included sweeping. Once we agreed, I set to work.

I cleaned out all the old newspapers and magazines and I threw them out the window to a trash bin down below. I picked up old toys, dusted off old antiques, and put fallen clothes back on their hangers. I didn't see Mrs. Hedaway for at least a couple of hours, that is until she brought me up a peanut butter sandwich and a glass of milk. With a quick comment on my wonderful work, she was gone again. Three hours later, I was done. I called to her and told her I was finished, so she came upstairs to inspect. "Great job," she commented.

"Can I have my money now?" I queried. "I want to get my new bike before the store closes." "Of course, young man. Hold on, and I will go and get my purse." When she returned, her face was kind of red and embarrassed. I knew something was wrong.

"I don't have your money," she said in a saddened voice. It seems that her son must have "borrowed" her cash and didn't tell her. I was devastated. "But you promised!" I shouted. "I just worked for five hours and I would like to get my money now." I knew that there was nothing she could say that would make me feel better, so I just put my head down between my hands and started to fake cry. *Ladies always go for that*, I thought to myself. *She'll find my money somehow.*

"Please don't cry. I'll tell you what. You can have anything up here in the attic that you want … anything!"

"Really?" I said. "Anything?"

I'll have to look around, I thought to myself. Maybe I could sell that bag of golf clubs, or that sewing machine. I was feeling a little better as I perused through all of her belongings and I finally asked about a small, strange looking wooden suitcase thing over on a shelf. "Oh, that's an old Victrola. It doesn't work, and there are parts missing," she said. "I'm sure you wouldn't want that old thing."

I didn't know what a Victrola was, but I was certainly interested. "It was made by the people who made Edison phonographs, but it was sold to a language school for students to borrow to listen to their lessons on it," she explained. "Sort of like library books. People would put these funny round records on the machine, crank it up, and stick some tubes in their ears to listen to their lessons."

The more she explained this contraption, the more I wanted it. She told me that her husband bought it at an estate sale a long time ago and that it'd been up in that attic for over forty years. Without even seeing it, I told her that I would take it in exchange for the money. I did find the missing horn for the "Language Phone" and located someone in a tiny repair shop in Boonton, New Jersey, who still had parts for it. It still plays great to this day. Not bad for something manufactured in 1890.

I did finally get my new bike, but it took me two more weekends of mowing lawns, digging a garden for Mrs. Horn, and robbing my brother Richard's sock drawer of $3.42.

Ask anyone I know, and they will tell you that I have a pretty good liking for cookies—all kinds, but especially Oreos. I'm not too crazy for all the silly flavor variations they seem to come up with just to sell more cookies, like watermelon, birthday cake, red velvet, and marshmallow fluff. The golden ones and the original ones are still the best.

My next favorite cookie is well, not a cookie at all, but a scone. I think they are in between a muffin and a cookie and there are so many variations that it's hard to choose a favorite. I found a recipe for just good old-fashioned vanilla scones, and after trying it out two or three times and making minor adjustments, I think I have come up with the most delicious and tastiest one of all. I have included some of my variations, and you can try them all and see which you like the best. One thing is for sure, you will probably be making these once a week if you have the same sweet tooth as I do.

VANILLA SCONES

2 3/4 cups all-purpose flour

1/3 cup sugar

3/4 teaspoon salt

1 tablespoon baking powder

1 stick cold, unsalted butter

2 eggs

2 teaspoons vanilla extract (other variations as needed)

Heavy whipping cream

Powdered sugar

Milk

Place the flour, sugar, and salt into a medium-sized bowl. Mix well. Add the baking powder and mix again. Cut up the butter into small chunks and add them to the flour mixture. Using a pastry cutter or two steak knives, cut the butter into the flour until you have very small, pea- sized chunks.

In a small measuring cup, crack the eggs and add the vanilla extract. If making any variation of the recipe, use the appropriate extract for that flavor (see variations below). Gently mix the eggs and vanilla and then add heavy cream until you have one-and-a-half cups of liquid. Mix well and pour into flour mixture. Use your hands to mix the dry ingredients with the liquids until blended. Do *not* overmix.

Preheat the oven to 425 degrees.

Line a 9x12 baking pan with parchment paper. Shape the dough on the pan and form a one-inch thick rectangle. Place the dough into a freezer and chill for about thirty minutes. Once removed from the freezer, shape the scones into small, two-inch squares and place them on the baking pan or use cookie cutters to make other shapes. Make sure the dough pieces are uniformly one inch thick. Brush the finished scones with milk. Bake for about twenty minutes, checking at the fifteen-minute mark for doneness. The bottoms should be slightly browned but not dark. Bake longer if necessary. Remove from the oven and let them cool for about twenty minutes.

Once the scones have cooled, make an icing using powdered sugar, whatever extract your scones have, and a little water. A thicker pasty icing is better than a watery dripping one. Use the back of a spoon to layer the icing and if you want, use a zester to add either orange or lemon zest to the tops of the frosted scones before they dry. Makes about 18 scones depending on size.

Variations:

Mix in small pieces of dried sweetened cranberries and a couple teaspoons of fresh orange zest from the peel of a navel orange to the wet ingredients before adding to the flour. Add additional orange zest to the top of a plain frosted scone while the icing is still wet.

Mix in some toasted almond slices and a teaspoon of almond extract to the wet ingredients before adding to the flour. Use some almond extract instead of vanilla in the icing.

Mix in some dried black cherries or tiny pieces of maraschino cherries into the wet liquid, a half-teaspoon of cherry or raspberry extract, and a drop of red food coloring before adding to the flour. Use the same cherry or raspberry extract in the icing with or without food coloring.

Mix in the zest of a small fresh lemon along with one-and-a-half teaspoons of lemon juice to the liquid ingredients before adding to the flour mixture. Add a couple of teaspoons of lemon juice to the icing along with a small drop of yellow food coloring. Shave a little lemon zest over the icing before it sets.

The baked and cooled scones can be frozen before frosting, or you can also freeze the dough wrapped tightly in plastic wrap. Just thaw it enough to roll it out on a parchment-laden baking pan.

Somehow, around Christmas time, I was always selected to put the lights on the tree. I wasn't sure why I got that job, but every year, it was nothing but a small nightmare. You see, come January 5, the tree had to come down and since the once fresh evergreen was up since the day after Thanksgiving, it was usually dry as a bone and you could use your breath to blow the needles off it. What I'm getting at is that taking it down was a huge mess. Everyone who helped would just yank off the ornaments and shove them in boxes. Then the lights would be pulled off in chunks and rolled up into a ball and put in another box. So, guess who had the pleasure of untangling the mess the following year? I did!

The whole family got involved in putting up the tree. After it was in the stand and fully secured, everyone waited for me to start putting on the lights. Of course, I was very meticulous about placing just the right number of bulbs on each branch and making sure there were no two green bulbs or red bulbs in a row because that just wouldn't do. I would stop after one strand, plug it in to make sure it was just right, and then unplug it and go on to the next. It usually took me a good two hours to get all the lights done and then everyone else could finish with the trimmings. My favorite part of lighting was putting in the bubble lights. We had about two dozen of these bulbs. They had a glass tube filled with some kind of colored alcohol and once the lamp gave off enough heat the fluid would bubble inside the glass tube and it would keep on bubbling and bubbling. I was so fascinated by the physics of those lights. When I got older and had my own apartment and my own tree, I started collecting these bubble lights to relive that wonderful childhood memory. Every year, even now in my 70's, I still enjoy sitting there in front of the tree and watching them bubble for hours on end. It's the small things in life, isn't it!

Here is a great dessert recipe you can make for a special dinner party, or instead of the usual two-layer birthday cake. There is a little "liquor" in it, so maybe it's best not to serve it to the kiddies. This is a make-ahead treat, so think ahead before making it.

ITALIAN RUM PUDDING CAKE

2 14-oz. packages Italian anisette sponge (not toast)

1/2 cup Bacardi Rum (dark or light)

1/2 cup sour cream

1 package of Jello Vanilla Instant Pudding

1 package of Jello Chocolate Instant Pudding

3-1/2 cups whole milk

1 cup heavy whipping cream

1 Hershey's Chocolate Bar, chilled

Optional: 1/2 cup slivered or sliced almonds, toasted

Using a 9-inch spring form pan, arrange the anisette sponge on the bottom of the pan with the side of the cookie facing up. Cut up more pieces to fill in any large gaps. Douse the sponge pieces with rum. Mix one-and-a-half cups of milk with the package of vanilla pudding and add the sour cream. Let the pudding set for about ten minutes. Pour the vanilla pudding over the rum doused cookies. Arrange another layer of anisette sponge over the vanilla pudding filling in any large gaps with extra pieces of cookie. Prepare the chocolate pudding with the other two cups of milk and let this stand about ten minutes to set. Pour the chocolate pudding over the second layer of anisette sponge. Cover the top with plastic wrap, directly on top of the pudding, and refrigerate overnight. Remove the outer form of the spring pan. Using a chilled deep bowl and beaters, whip the heavy cream for two minutes. Add a couple tablespoons of sugar and continue whipping until slightly stiff peaks form. Spread the whipped topping over the chocolate pudding. Using a medium cut cheese grater, grate the chilled chocolate bar over the whipped cream or you can just sift chocolate drink mix over the top layer. Add the toasted almond slices, if desired. Chill before serving. This recipe makes about 10 servings.

Kids today don't realize just how good they have it sometimes. They have more fancy electronic toys and gadgets to keep them occupied nowadays than we ever had growing up.

Everything is done on Wi-Fi—no wires, no bulky converters to set up, and most of all, they have access to hundreds of channels of entertainment right at their fingertips.

We grew up with VHF television and we were lucky if we got six channels. I remember way back in 1965 when we got our first color TV. It was a huge, round, 21-inch screen—the biggest in the industry at the time. It was hooked up to an antenna on the roof and that antenna was at the mercy of any thunder and lightning storm, heavy rains, summer and fall windstorms, and of course, winter snow and ice storms. Invariably if the elements were just right, the darn antenna would fall down onto the roof and there would go the TV reception. When this happened, someone (usually me and my brothers) would have to climb up onto the roof and fix it. This meant risking my skinny, fragile, bony body to sudden death if I were to slip on the icy roof or snow-packed eaves. Once on the roof I would survey the damage, then climb back down and head to the hardware store to fetch yet another metal pole, or another set of chimney straps to fix the darn thing. After making the repairs, one of us would go into the living room and start clicking the TV channel dial around to see how many decent pictures we could get with minimum distortion. Most of the time, channel 2 would be clear and channel 4 would be fuzzy. Channel 7 had shadows and channel 9 had snow. So, my helper would rush outside and yell to me to turn the antenna to the right or left or completely around the other way. This could sometimes take hours just to get all six channels to come in as clearly as possible. When it was as good as it would get, I would call it quits and climb back down. My reward was to watch some great sitcoms like *Bewitched*, *I Dream of Jeannie*, *Gilligan's Island*, and *Flipper*, and some of them were broadcast in "Living Color." Oh, *TV Guide Magazine* was only 15 cents then, too.

AUNT YOLANDA'S ITALIAN ANISE COOKIES

<u>For the Dough:</u>

3/4 cup sugar
1 stick un-salted butter (melted)
2 large eggs, at room temperature
1/4 cup whole milk
1 teaspoon anise extract
3-1/4 cups all-purpose flour
2-1/2 teaspoons baking powder
1/4 teaspoon salt

Beat the first five ingredients together in a large mixing bowl using a stand mixer on low speed.

Mix the flour, baking powder, and salt in a smaller bowl and then add this to the butter mixture and mix thoroughly by hand. Wrap the dough in plastic wrap and refrigerate for approximately thirty minutes. Preheat the oven to 325 degrees.

Uncover the dough and drop rounded teaspoonfuls of dough onto a pre-greased baking sheet, one inch apart. You can also roll the dough out and twist into shapes as shown in the photo.

Bake for twelve minutes. The bottoms of the cookies should be lightly browned. Remove them from the oven and let them sit for about two minutes; then transfer them to a wire rack to cool completely.

<u>For the Icing:</u>

1 cup confectioners' sugar
7 tablespoons milk
1 teaspoon anise extract

In a small narrow bowl, stir the three ingredients together until smooth. Dip the cookie tops into the icing and let them dry on the wire rack lined underneath with paper towels or wax paper. Quickly sprinkle the cookies with nonpareils (sprinkles) before the icing sets. Depending on the size of the cookie, you may get about five dozen from this recipe. You can also tint the icing with red and green food coloring and make colorful Christmas cookies.

HOLY EGGS

One summer, I got the chance to go visit my grandparent's (my dad's side) who lived in upstate New York in a little town called Carthage. I stayed with them for a couple of weeks. They had a huge house with three floors, and a large back yard where they raised peacocks, pigs, and chickens. About thirty feet from the front door were railroad tracks that crossed in front of their house on an angle. I remember being awakened in the middle of the night sometimes when a freight train would rumble through carrying coal. I would get out of bed when I heard the locomotive whistle blow and sit by the bedroom window on the second floor to count the cars as they passed by. Sometimes, I counted over a hundred coal cars. FYI: I love trains!

My grandfather grew lots of vegetables in his garden out back. Sometimes I would help him till the soil and pick weeds for him, but we hardly ever spoke. I don't think he knew much English.

One morning, I got up early and came down to the kitchen where I watched my grandmother making my grandpa's breakfast. She sliced up some Italian bread and spread oleo margarine on both sides of the bread and then popped them onto a hot frying pan. After they were toasted on the one side, she would get a 1 to 2-inch glass and cut out the center of the bread. She then cracked open an egg and placed it in the center of the bread. She added a bit of salt and pepper to them, turned down the heat, and left. After about ten minutes, she returned and then flipped the bread pieces over on the other side. Then she left again. A timer went off and grandpa came into the kitchen, grabbed himself a cup of hot, fresh coffee, and sat down to these wonderful egg/toast concoctions. I thought it was a strange way of serving eggs, but it stuck in my head. I tried them a few times when I had some bread about to go stale. They were pretty good, even better served with a bit of Tabasco sauce and tomato slices on the side. Anyway, I thought I would share that little bit of history about my grandparents. Oh, if you happen to see the movie *Moonstruck*, you'll see Olympia Dukakis making Holy Eggs for her father, the older Italian guy in the movie, who also doesn't talk much.

Here's what you need to make them! Read through the story and prepare them just as my grandmother did. ENJOY!

Eggs
Oleo margarine or butter
Large loaf of Italian bread, cut into 1-inch slices
Salt and pepper
Optional ingredients: tomato slices and Tabasco Sauce

As I mentioned earlier, chemistry was always my favorite subject in school. I loved going to chemistry class and learning all about the elements and how stuff is changed from one form to another. I always had an interest in becoming a scientist someday. That was, up until I nearly blew up the basement and almost ended the lives of my parents and at least three of the kids.

I was "fooling around" with my chemistry set in the corner of the basement one night, while everyone as asleep. I mixed a couple of things I shouldn't have, and a plume of thick white and gray smoke started flowing up from the glass beaker. Within minutes, I was coughing, choking, and wheezing. Of course, the only window in the basement was in the laundry room so I rushed in there, climbed onto the washer, and tried to pry it open. The latch was so rusted that it wouldn't open, but it was too late anyway. The heavy smoke had gone right up through the ventilator into my parent's bedroom. Dad came rushing downstairs in his undershorts with a broom and it's easy to pretty much guess what happened next. All my glassware, chemicals, and test tubes wound up in the trash and I was told never to "experiment" ever again. It took us two days to get the smell of rotten eggs out of the house.

About a year later, my father came home with a whole box of old chemistry equipment he had gotten from a retired doctor he knew. He said I could set up my laboratory once again but only in the garage outside. I was back to being an amateur chemist, and it wasn't long before I ran out of unbroken glassware.

My friend Billy knew of this pharmaceutical company in the next town over that "threw away" all of their laboratory glassware every Saturday. So, he and I got on our bikes and headed for the hills of Holmdel. The S.S. White Pharmaceutical Company was huge. There were about six buildings on the complex and we rode around for a good half hour before we found the labs. Sure enough, out back near the trash were boxes and boxes of discarded flasks, test tubes, condenser tubes– you name it. We hit the jackpot. One thing we forgot to bring was something to carry all our loot home in. I decided that we should tuck our tee shirts into our pants and stuff our shirts full of the glassware. We looked like a couple of pregnant ladies with all the wrong bulges. So, off we went on our bikes, heading home when the worst thing happened. I started to gain a lot of speed going down one of the long hills, so I put on my front brake by mistake and the brake pad broke off and got stuck in the front rim. The bike screeched to a stop, and I went flying over the handlebars, landing on the graveled pavement face-first. The glassware under my shirt smashed into a million pieces and tore into my entire torso as I skidded down the road. I was lucky that Billy wasn't far behind, as he saw the whole thing and he helped by dragging my bloody body up a small hill to the closest house available. I was in a daze. Billy rang the doorbell and a lady answered the door. She gasped in fright as she saw me and the trail of blood I was leaving all over her nice clean porch. After he explained what happened, she called for an ambulance and told Billy to keep me off her brand-new white carpet.

I recovered in the ER, and they told me they removed about 200 pieces of glass from my body. I was wrapped like a mummy and remained that way for the next two weeks. It was tough eating and going to the bathroom, but I made it through okay.

I still have about six pieces of glassware from my childhood lab that I keep around to remind me of that horrible incident and my decision to become a kitchen scientist instead of a research one. To me cooking ***is*** a type of chemistry. You get to add ingredients, take chances, and try to create something that is both tasty and wonderful. That's why I love cooking so much; you can be creative, imaginative, resourceful with meats, herbs and veggies, and still produce something that doesn't kill people ***or*** smell like rotten eggs.

Here is a recipe for one of my favorite cookies—and it's so easy, too!

CARAMEL COATED SHORTBREAD

2 sticks soft butter
1/2 cup confectioners' sugar
1/2 teaspoon salt
2 1/4 cups all-purpose flour
1/2 teaspoon baking powder
1/8 teaspoon vanilla extract

For the Coating:

10-15 caramels
1/3 cup heavy cream

Preheat the oven to 350 degrees. Cream the butter with the confectioner's sugar until it's smooth. Add the salt and flour, along with the baking powder and vanilla. You can use a pastry cutter to combine these ingredients. Once all the flour is incorporated, turn the crumbly mixture out into a square or round metal skillet that is oven safe. Press down the dough until it is smooth all around. Make sure it is uniformly thick. Once it is all pressed down flat, use a fork to prick holes in the entire surface. Use a sharp steak knife to score lines into the dough. If using a round pan, make the "pizza" sliced pieces about two inches at the edge. You don't need to cut completely through the dough; just score it to about one-sixteenth. Bake in the Preheated oven for about twenty minutes or until the tops just start getting brown. Remove from oven and let the cookies cool.

Combine the caramels and cream in a small saucepan over low heat until they melt. Stir and drizzle over the cooled shortbread. You can also use a microwave to do this: two minutes on medium power. Stir and repeat if needed. Makes about 20 pieces depending on size.

If you asked any New Jersey sixth grader in the 1960s what the state bird of New Jersey was, they would snicker and say, "the mosquito." New Jersey gets a lot of rain. In the spring, summer and fall—constant rain. This was fine except that the pools of water that stood around in the muggy wet air bred the largest variety of mosquitoes known to man. Once they became intolerable, one could expect a visit from the city exterminator, whom we called "The Mosquito Man." This guy would come around with a big truck, similar to a fire truck, and he would go up and down the streets and spray insecticide fog into the air. His hope was to kill the thousands of bugs that disturbed everyone's BBQs, backyard picnics, and baseball games. We never knew when he would show up and it was usually unexpected. Of course, we kids would run after the truck and play in the foggy mist that spewed from the back of the truck until it evaporated. Who knew what was in that stuff, but as a kid you didn't care about that. We just cared that it was fun. Once in a while we'd cough or choke, and it was clear we'd had enough.

Our summer weekends usually started out by inviting as many family members as we could get in touch with to a backyard picnic. There would be the usual hot dogs, hamburgers, and sausages, but the thing I remember most about our cookouts was the large pot of Giambotta (pronounced GEE-UM-BOTTA). This vegetable and hot dog stew is simple and very economical to make, especially if you have a nice vegetable garden as we always did growing up. Loosely translated, Giambotta means "a mess of everything."

GIAMBOTTA

1/2 lb. string beans, blanched

3 or 4 small zucchini, un-peeled and cut into slices

1 each red and green pepper

1/2 large onion

3-4 garlic cloves

4 medium-sized potatoes, peeled

1 lb. hot dogs, cut into small pieces

1 large can of crushed tomatoes

1 large can of tomato puree

4-5 fresh basil leaves, cut up

Salt and pepper to taste

Start by blanching the string beans in boiling water for about five minutes. Drain and set aside. Cut up all the other vegetables into chunks and set them aside. Put some olive oil in a large Dutch oven and sauté the garlic for a few minutes (not too brown). Add the cans of tomatoes and a little water. Place all the veggies in the pot. Lastly, add the cut up hot dogs and the basil leaves. Cover and simmer on medium heat for about twenty-five minutes. Add some salt and pepper to taste. To spice things up a bit more, add some crushed red pepper flakes to the mix. This is a great summertime stew, but it is also great on a cold, wet, snowy winter evening. This recipe will serve at least 10 hungry people.

I loved reading comic books as a kid in the 1950s. Superman action comics were my favorite. I collected a lot of them and I'm sure if I still had them to this day, they would be worth some big bucks. But as most kids did back then, we traded them with friends for other things like a stupid whiffle ball or a pair of rusted ice skates.

Once in a while I would glance at the back page of the comic book and there would be a ton of ads selling everything from "Sea Monkeys" to "X-Ray glasses." One particular ad caught my eye and so I cut it out and put it away in my desk. It was for a "Haunted House Mystery Bank." I remember reading the ad over and over again because I was intrigued as to how it worked. Here's what it said:

If you like chills and thrills of the unusual, then this bank is for you. It makes saving your money real fun too. Just place a penny, nickel, dime or if you are really rich, a quarter, on the doorstep of the house. With a groan and a rattle, the door spookily opens. The house shutters and quakes. The horror hand sneaks out of the doorway and snatches the coin and drags it into the house. The door slams shut, and all is quiet again.

They really made it sound so mysterious and sinister. I had to have it. "Wow," I thought, "it was only $5.95 plus 35 cents for postage and handling." I wasn't sure what handling was, but it still sounded like a bargain. So, I raided my sister Celia's eyeglass case in the back of my sock drawer and counted my money. I had over $7. With mom's help, we taped the coins and dollar bills to a piece of paper and the ad and sent it in to Honor House Products of New York.

Every day for two weeks I rushed out to the postman and asked him if he had my package from New York. "Not yet, sonny. Maybe tomorrow!"

My haunted house bank finally arrived, and I rushed upstairs to my bedroom and tore open the packing. I pulled the box out and opened it. I was immediately disappointed because the mysterious ghost ridden house was only seven inches tall. "What a gyp," I thought.

Then I grabbed the packing receipt in the box and looked over that ad again. That's when I noticed the size: 7x7x4. Now, I wouldn't have been that surprised but I read that ad repeatedly until I memorized it, never noticing the size of the toy.

In a few minutes, I had the bank opened, installed the two AA batteries, and started searching around my room for a coin. I found a penny in the corner near my bed and picked it up, rushed over to my bank, and popped the coin down on the doorstep. After a few seconds, a tiny squeak sounded, then a clunking noise, and then the door opened. As promised, a tiny skeleton hand reached out, grabbed the penny, and slid it into its house. "Where was all that horrifying quaking and rattling?" I asked myself. This was nothing like I thought it would be. I repeated my original disappointment: "What a gyp."

After realizing that I spent my hard-earned money on a piece of junk, I decided I needed to do something to break even. I took my bank to school and after describing the mysterious bank with its chills and spills to my friends, I had them all dying to try it. Out came their dimes, nickels, and quarters. Most of the kids loved it so much they tried it again and again. After about a week, I took the bank home and counted my money. I had over $12 and change.

I guess the toy wasn't a gyp after all, but it did teach me a valuable lesson. Always read the fine print.

Kitchen Tip: Run a knife under hot water before slicing a cheesecake, moist chocolate cake, or any food that might be sticky. You will get nice clean edges.

Many Italians, or non-Italians for that matter, have never heard of nor had Bolognese Sauce. This is a versatile vegetable-based sauce that has a lot of wonderful uses. You can use this sauce to liven up eggplant parmesan, to spice up a vegetable lasagna, or to use directly on top of any type of pasta. You can sauté chicken breasts or veal medallions with this sauce and the taste will be nothing like you've ever had before. Get adventurous.

LEN'S BOLOGNESE SAUCE

4-6 garlic cloves, minced
3/4 cup olive oil
1 medium onion (cut into small chunks)
3-4 medium carrots (peeled and cut into 1" chunks)
3-4 stalks celery (cut into 3" pieces)
1/2 cup water
1 12-oz. container table cream
8-10 large fresh basil leaves, minced
1-2 tablespoons salt (or to taste)
1 cup chardonnay (or other dry white wine)
1/4 teaspoon oregano
2 large cans of crushed tomatoes

In a large pot, place the minced garlic and the olive oil and heat on low to medium heat.

Sauté the garlic for about five minutes, but do not let the pieces get brown. Remove from heat.

Attach the "fine shredding" blade to a food processor then shred the veggies. Reheat the oil/garlic blend and add the shredded vegetables.

Add more oil if necessary and sauté on low heat for about five minutes, stirring occasionally.

Add the two cans of tomatoes and the water. Add the wine, the minced basil leaves, and the oregano. Add salt to taste. Cook on low heat for about two hours, stirring occasionally. At about the 90-minute mark, add the table cream and stir well. This recipe will yield about 2 quarts of prepared sauce.

The sauce is now ready to use, but if to make it into a chicken dish, try the following.

Cut two medium chicken breasts into quarter-inch slices. In a frying pan, add about a quarter cup of olive oil and one-half stick of butter. Once the butter is melted, lay the chicken strips into the pan. Sauté them until they are no longer pink. Add the chicken pieces and all the oil/juices right into the pot of Bolognese sauce and cook an additional thirty minutes. Serve this chicken over some penne or ziti pasta sprinkled with grated cheese and with some garlic bread. If there is any chardonnay left over, serve it with dinner as well. Buon Appetite.

Another variation for this great sauce is Eggplant Bolognese. Here is the recipe for that.

EGGPLANT BOLOGNESE

2 quarts prepared Bolognese Sauce
Olive oil for frying
2 large or 3 medium eggplants
3 eggs (for the ricotta filling)
2-3 eggs for coating the eggplant, beaten
1 large 32-oz. container of whole milk ricotta
Fresh parsley
Salt and pepper
Grated cheese
Italian seasoned breadcrumbs
1 lb. shredded mozzarella cheese

Prepare the ricotta cheese: In a large bowl, mix the ricotta, three eggs, about two tablespoons of fresh parsley, and three or four tablespoons of grated cheese. Add a pinch of salt and pepper to taste. Mix until smooth and set aside.

Peel the eggplant and cut into quarter-inch slices. Preheat a deep fry pan with some olive oil, about one-eighth inch deep.

In a deep wide bowl, beat the other eggs. Place a nice layer of breadcrumbs in another flat plate. Coat each piece of eggplant in the egg mixture a few times on each side and place them into the breadcrumbs. Again, coat each side once or twice. Place them into the fry pan and cook until they are lightly browned on both sides. Place the fried pieces between paper towels to soak up any oil. Add more pieces as you take them out. After about fifteen pieces, you may want to drain this oil, wipe the pan, and start again with fresh oil. The breadcrumbs tend to burn easily.

Take a good-sized glass lasagna pan and coat the bottom with a little olive oil. Lay the eggplant slices on the bottom of the pan. Layer some Bolognese sauce over each piece of eggplant. Add another layer of eggplant slices and more sauce over this layer. Spread the prepared ricotta cheese over the second layer and then sprinkle the shredded mozzarella cheese over the ricotta. Layer more sauce over this layer and add the final layer of eggplant slices. Cover the top with more Bolognese sauce and some grated cheese. Bake in a 375-degree oven for about 90 minutes, or until the sauce bubbles in the center of the pan. Let sit for about fifteen minutes before serving. This recipe will make about 10 servings.

This sauce can be placed in a zip lock freezer bag and frozen for two to three months. You can defrost it right in the plastic bag on the counter or cut the frozen sauce into chunks and defrost in a microwave oven on a low power setting.

Almost every family I have ever known has had at least one person who was just a bit strange. I'm not saying that in a derogatory way, but there was always that one aunt, uncle, or cousin who just "stood out." Our Uncle Charlie was the one in our family. We didn't see Uncle Charlie much. Some would tell us that he was locked up for being a bit "crazy." Others said that he was the one brother of my grandmother who couldn't communicate much because he was "slow." Another story was that he came over on the boat from the motherland and never knew how to speak any English.

What I do remember about good old Uncle Charlie was that whenever he visited, he always showed up with a gallon jug of red chianti. I can still picture him sitting there I the corner of the backyard tucked away from all the activity, occasionally taking a slug from that wine bottle and quietly watching everything that went on. He had on his signature fedora hat and sticking out of his mouth was one of those awful smelling stogie cigars.

Once when I was about 10, we were having a cookout in the back yard, and I once again noticed good ol' Uncle Charlie and right next to him was that gallon of Carlo Rossi Chianti. Now, we kids weren't allowed to drink wine. The grown-ups told us it would stunt our growth. As I watched Uncle Charlie, I realized that since he didn't speak, he couldn't refuse me any wine. So, I grabbed a small paper cup and wandered over to him. Making sure there was no one else around, I motioned for him to pour me a little wine in my cup and sure enough, he did. I sat down in the dirt next to him and cupped the wine between my legs. My first swig was interesting. I both liked it and hated it. I guess wine had to grow on you. After about three sips, I stood up and got a bit tipsy. I weighed all of about fifty pounds and that wine went straight to my head. I managed to get my footing and turned around to hear Uncle Charlie mumble something in Italian: "Il bambino, pazzo." I later learned that he called me a stupid little boy.

Gus watching over the wine

Well, I finally did find out that he could speak, just not *my* language.

Here in the age of the Internet, a person can surf for hours and hours and maybe come up with at least three dozen recipes for cheesecake.

Cheesecake is one of those Italian favorites you just can't pass up on the dessert menu. I have made many of them in my lifetime and I keep coming back to my old favorite– a recipe that my dad used in his restaurant. This one is nice and creamy with hints of orange, lemon, and vanilla.

LEN'S CREAMY ITALIAN CHEESECAKE

2 packages (8 oz.) Philadelphia cream cheese (not low fat), at room temp

1 15-oz. container of whole milk ricotta cheese

1-pint sour cream

1 stick unsalted butter, melted and cooled

3 tablespoons corn starch

3 tablespoons all-purpose flour

4 large eggs, room temp

1-1/2 cups sugar

2 tablespoons vanilla extract (not imitation)

The rind from half a large lemon

The rind from half a large navel orange

2 tablespoons lemon juice

In a large glass bowl, mix the ricotta and the cream cheese using a mixer on medium speed until smooth and free of lumps. Add the sugar, eggs, lemon juice, vanilla, cornstarch, and flour. Mix for about two minutes on high. Add the melted butter and rinds. Lastly, add the sour cream and mix well. Pour into a greased 10-inch springform pan. Place the pan onto a large piece of heavy-duty aluminum foil and wrap it so that it comes up about three inches on the sides.

Preheat the oven to 350 degrees. Place the foil prepared pan into a large roasting pan and pour hot water into the outer pan coming up about half the width of the foil. Bake for about fifty minutes, then check for slight browning on top. If it is very light brown, and still "jiggly" in the center, open the oven door for about thirty seconds, close the door, and turn off the heat. Let the cake continue baking for another thirty minutes and check to see if the center is firm by slightly jarring the cake pan. Remove the cake from the oven and remove the side of the springform. Cover the cake with plastic wrap and place in a refrigerator for a couple of hours.

Top the cheesecake with cherry or blueberry pie filling or sprinkle powdered sugar on it before serving with no filling.

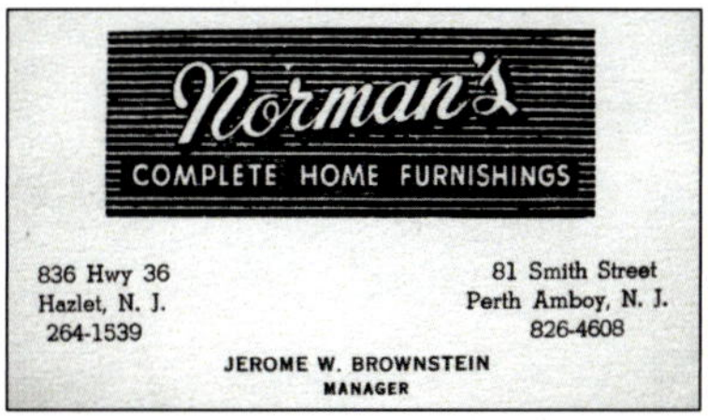

My mother always cringed when the sixth day of the month rolled around. That was the day that Norman Schneiderman usually showed up for money. Norman was the "Silas Marner" of the business world. He owned Norman's Complete Home Furnishings Store in Hazlet, New Jersey. Mom made the mistake of buying some furniture from him on "time." Back then, if a person didn't have a lot of cash, some stores would offer credit terms and customers paid their balance either weekly or monthly. This was also before credit cards.

So, on that sixth day of the month, Norman would make his rounds and go to people's houses to collect his money. Mom would remember he was about to show up and would frantically run all around the house closing drapes, pulling down shades, shutting off all lights, and herding all the kids under their beds to make it look like nobody was at home.

Of course, this particular Tuesday we were having chicken and sausage penne primavera. You could smell those sausages cooking from three blocks away.

Well, the old black Cadillac El Dorado pulled up in front of the house and Norman got out of the car. He walked up to the house and started knocking on the door. "I know you're home, Mary!" I can smell that I-talian food! I need some money, Mary! I know you're in there!"

After a few more knocks, mom would open the door and let old snide and deceitful Norman in. She would rummage through her pocketbook and pull out some bills. Norman would just stand there like a hoodlum and wait while she counted out mostly one-dollar bills. Norman would scrounge around in his suit pocket and pull out a piece of wrinkled paper to scribble on it how much she had paid then hand it to her. It was a half a napkin one time, and an old gas station receipt the next. My mother would just take the receipts and put them in an old shoe box in the closet.

One day about two years later, I found that box of receipts and questioned mom about all the money she had given him over the years. I said to her that she should have paid off this furniture a long time ago. She found the original bill and I made some calculations. Sure enough, adding all the crumpled-up receipts and payments, she had paid for the furniture one-and-a-half times over.

The next time ol' Norman showed up, I was there, and I let him have it. I flashed all the receipts in his face and told him he wasn't getting another nickel from us for his lousy furniture. He was done scamming us. Needless to say, we never saw hide nor hair of him ever again.

In memory of good ol' Norman, here is my recipe for Chicken and Sausage Penne Primavera.

CHICKEN & SAUSAGE PENNE PRIMAVERA

1-2 chicken breasts, cut into bite-sized pieces
2-3 links mild Italian sausage
1 red pepper, sliced thin
1 large can of chopped or diced tomatoes, with juice
3-4 cloves garlic
1 large can of low-sodium chicken broth
1/2 pint half-and-half or table cream
1 lb. penne pasta, cooked al-dente
1 cup rosé wine
3/4 cup shredded mozzarella
Pinch of oregano
Pinch of dry basil
Black pepper
1/8 cup olive oil
3-4 pats of butter
Optional ingredient: Crushed red pepper flakes

Cook the pasta al-dente and set aside. Put the olive oil and butter in a nice sized deep casserole pan and sauté the garlic. After a few minutes, add the chicken chunks and the sausage links. Once the sausage is browned, remove from the pot and cut them into small slices and return them to the pot. Cook for another seven to eight minutes and then remove the meats and set them aside. Add the red peppers, the can of tomatoes, and their juices. Add the spices and chicken broth. Bring this to a boil. Add the rosé wine and simmer another five or so minutes. Add the table cream and mix until the sauce thickens. Do not boil. Return the meats to the pot and add the crushed red pepper, if desired. Add the cooked pasta and continue heating until everything is nice and hot. Add the mozzarella cheese just before serving. Feeds about 6 people depending on the size of the chicken breasts used.

The funeral home was a strange place to bring a kid, of any age. When my dad died in 1965, we had to make funeral arrangements, so mom asked my oldest sister, Celia, to take her to John Muhlenbeck's Funeral Home. John was a friend and poker buddy of my father's, so we had seen him once or twice at the house.

When we arrived, we were greeted by a nice receptionist who led us into a fancy parlor strewn with plush red velvet chairs and heavy drapes with huge ropes tied to them. There were some caskets on stands with their lids opened and lights shining on the insides. Although I was 17, I had never been inside a funeral home or been that close to a casket, for that matter. It was kind of eerie.

Mom got busy chatting with John, and I got a bit fidgety sitting there, so I decided to wander around. I walked out of that room and down a long hallway and into another room. The door was marked with a giant C-1. I felt like I was on the *Price Is Right* and there were luxurious prizes behind it. I pushed it open and immediately three dimly lit florescent lights went on. One of them started buzzing. I looked around and saw four huge refrigerators with steel doors. I figured that this is where they kept all the wine, beer, and soft drinks for visitors, so I went over and opened one up. Inside were long trays with dead bodies on them, all covered in plastic. I nearly had a coronary myself and slammed the door shut. I guess curiosity got the best of me and after a minute or two, I decided to check them out a bit more. I opened the second ice box and sure enough, more bodies. I just had to poke one of them just to feel the chill of frosted flesh. I reached under the plastic and pushed my finger into someone's leg. It felt like a frozen Twinkie, not quite solid, but cake-like and cold. Then I noticed the toe tag. Again, my curiosity took over and I pulled on the tag, turned it over and read it. "Mr. Wallace S. Simmons" it read, "died on March 1st, 1965 … COD COR THROM. Male 87 YR."

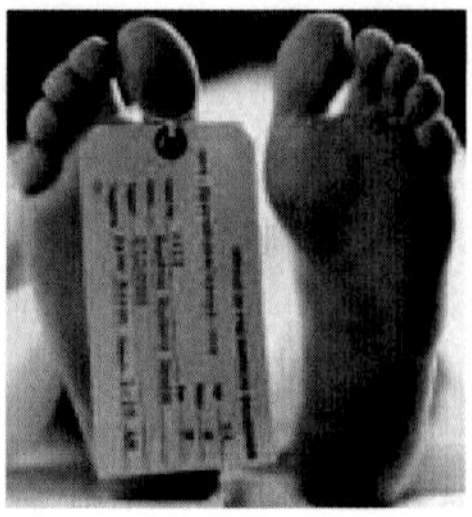

I wasn't quite sure what all that meant so I just covered him back up and closed the door. I turned to walk out of the room and just then the door opened and in walked a young man in a lab coat. There was nowhere to go, so I just stood there and froze solid like Mr. Simmons. "You're not allowed in here, mister," he yelled. "This is off limits to the public!"

I quickly yelled back, "Sorry!" then started toward the door. The guy turned back to me and said, "No, don't go. I'm sorry I yelled. Stay and chat with me." I said, "Okay, but just for a little while. My mom is probably ready to go!"

We exchanged names and I asked about his job as an undertaker and what it was like being around all these dead people all the time. He commented that he preferred this job because it was always quiet, no one bothered him, and his "customers" never complain. "How morbid," I thought. Being around all this death would make me go insane, but to each his own. Someone has to do it. Finally, I asked him about the toe tag. He said, "COD means cause of death, and COR Throm meant he died of coronary thrombosis– sort of like a heart attack. It happens to a lot of older folks."

"The pay is good," he added. "Well," I said, "I need to go, but just one more question: What do you tell people when they ask where you work?" He smiled and said, "I just tell them I work in the filling and packaging department."

If there is one thing I know, it's that anything chocolate will wipe away tears, soothe the pain of a bruised knee, and make the fact that you weren't chosen for the little league baseball team feel a bit better. I wasn't very good at contact sports. I couldn't throw a curve ball to save my life. I couldn't go deep for a pass if there was a hundred-dollar bill waiting for me at the goal post. What I was good at was gymnastics. I was great on the rings, terrific on the pommel horse, and I really excelled at climbing the ropes.

One day during gym class, I had snuck in a Hershey Bar in my gym shorts and was quietly eating it while watching my classmates climbing the ropes. I didn't think for one moment that I would be called on since it was about two minutes until class ended. But, as luck would have it, I was. There I stood with gooey, chocolate-covered fingers and no place to wipe them clean. I tried to lick them, but it was taking too much time, so I reached into my gym shorts and wiped off the chocolate on my nice clean Fruit of the Loom briefs. Ah, no one was the wiser.

After gym class, I went about the rest of my day. Later that evening I dropped my gym bag on the floor of my room as I always did. Little did I know that my sister was doing a load of laundry and went hunting all around the house for enough clothes to do a load. It didn't take long for her to find my chocolate stained underwear and make me the laughing stock of the entire family at dinner. You can imagine what was implied, can't you? I never did live that one down.

Here is one of my favorite ways to use chocolate.

CHOCOLATE CHOCOLATE CHIP COOKIES

3/4 cup butter unsalted, at room temp
3/4 cup sugar
1/2 cup light brown sugar
1 teaspoon vanilla extract
2 large eggs
1-3/4 cups all-purpose flour
1/2 cup Hershey's Special Dark Cocoa
3/4 teaspoon baking soda
1/2 teaspoon baking powder
1-1/2 cups Hershey's Semi-Sweet Mini Chocolate Chips
Pinch of salt

Get two bowls, one large and one small. In the small bowl, add butter and the sugars. Beat with an electric mixer until creamy. Add the eggs one at a time and then add the vanilla. Beat for about two minutes. In the other bowl, add the flour, cocoa, baking powder, baking soda plus a pinch of salt. Using a wooden spoon, add the cocoa flour mixture to the butter mixture and just combine. Try not to over beat the dough. Add the chocolate chips and again, just mix until combined. Chill the dough for about thirty minutes. Use a rounded tablespoon or a heaping teaspoon and drop onto a parchment-lined baking pan. Leave about two inches all around. Bake at 375 degrees for about eight minutes or a bit longer until the center is set. Remove from oven and let cool about five minutes. Remove from pan and cool completely on a wire rack. Makes about 3 dozen large cookies.

One day in early November 1961, my dad came home with a paper grocery sack filled with some oranges, lemons, a bottle of rye whiskey, and a mesh bag of candy on a string. Being the curious one of the bunch, I watched and listened as he explained how he was going to make a special liquor which also doubled as medicine. Now more curious than ever, I had to watch every step. He got out an old quart mason jar and filled it with rock candy. This was like diamonds of sugar on a string. Next, he cut up some navel oranges and lemons and added them to the jar along with some cherries and grapes. Once he couldn't fit another thing into the jar, he started pouring in the rye whiskey. When it was full, he put the lid on it, tightened it, and placed it in the brown paper bag. "Here it must sit for at least six months," he said. He took the jar and opened up a locked cabinet in the dining room. He placed the jar in there and took out one that he had made last year. There wasn't much left in the jar, but he gave me a taste. It was thick like melted jelly and tasted like Vick's Vapor Rub. I guess you had to get used to it.

When I got older, I found an old Rock 'n Rye decanter at an antique store for a quarter and brought it. It was empty but it brought back that memory of my dad making that Rock 'n Rye so I thought I would try it. I found out that it's also used to treat a sore throat, minor colds, fevers, and body aches. I've included the recipe as I remember it from my dad. Try it! If nothing else, it makes for an interesting and different cordial drink at your next dinner party.

ROCK AND RYE

1 small lemon, cut into wedges
1 navel orange (thick skinned), cut into eighths
Red and green maraschino cherries
A handful of red or white seedless grapes
A quart of cheap rye whiskey
1 box of rock candy (get this at an Asian or Korean market)

Read the story above and it's clear how to make it. Have fun!

About three weeks before Christmas, the mailman would deliver the Sears *Christmas Wish Book*. In our house it was just like winning the lottery. All us kids would sit around the dining room table and we would pass the book around. We would get to pick out one "big" gift as mom called it. When my turn came, I frantically flipped through all the pages hoping to find the one and only gift I wanted: a three-stage Atlas Model Rocket with re-entry parachute. Ever since I had seen the commercial while watching *I Dream of Jeannie*, I myself "dreamt" of owning one of my own.

My brother already ear-marked the page "Toys for Boys," so I quickly pulled open the page and started to scan the pictures. Fire engines, ice skates, tinker toys, erector sets, Lionel trains, hula hoops … no rockets. Next page, nothing.

After the final page, I started back at the beginning thinking I somehow overlooked the rocket section.

Apparently, Sears wanted to disappoint lots of little boys at Christmas because they neglected to include rockets in their special wish book.

I decided I wasn't going to settle for a lousy red-rider BB gun, or a Hop-Along Cassidy coonskin cap. My disappointment turned into desperation. I figured that if Sears didn't have a rocket, perhaps Montgomery Wards would.

The next day, I waited out on the front porch until the mailman pulled up. I ran to greet him and asked if he happened to have the Montgomery Ward version of the Christmas wish books. As it turned out he did, but he told me it belonged to Mr. Flagler down the street and he couldn't even let me look at it. "It's a crime for me to knowingly deliver the mail to the wrong person," he said. I could get in a heap of trouble.

Two days later, I walked over to see my neighbor Mr. Flagler. After explaining my dilemma, he was excited to give me his copy. I sat down in the living room and he came in and handed me the catalog. I was filled with hope as I thumbed through page after page. Finally, on page 82, there it was. Revell's three-stage Atlas Model Rocket with parachute landing spaceman. With his permission, I tore out the page and ran home. All the kids had their "big" gift circled and Mom had the catalog. I gave her my page and she added it to the others.

Christmas morning was as chaotic as usual, as we picked out brightly wrapped packages and tore into them with wild abandon. Trying to keep nine kids calm was out of the question. With paper wrappings strewn all about, string and bows everywhere, it was a free for all for the next hour. I got a scarf, a package of underwear, a pair of Snap-On goulashes, and a really neat shiny headlight for my bike-- but no rocket.

As Christmas day wore on, my sulking waned as well, and by dinner time, I had completely forgotten about the rocket. We ate, watched *Frosty the Snowman* and *Rudolph the Red Nosed Reindeer* on TV and by 7:30 pm I was ready for bed.

I climbed the stairs and opened my bedroom door. I walked over to my bed only to find my brother tucked completely under the covers sleeping there. I became a little miffed and started pushing against him. To my surprise, it wasn't my brother at all. I pulled back the covers to reveal the really huge box containing a big giant Atlas three-stage rocket. I stood there with tears of happiness running down my face and turned around to see my mother at the door to my room.

"Your 'big' gift was just *too* big to fit under the tree. Merry Christmas, son."

I am still amazed that I am still alive to write some of these stories of my childhood. By all standards, I should be dead. My brothers and I would play cowboys and Indians in the back yard, and we had some toy weapons that today wouldn't be allowed on toy store shelves. I had a bow and arrow that shot wooden dowels with rubber tips on them. After a few flights across the yard, the tips would go missing but that didn't keep us from shooting them again and again at live human targets. Luckily, I still have both my eyes and my ten toes and fingers.

In our old neighborhood there was a construction site. Over the course of three seasons, a nearby small retention ditch grew in size until it was a huge, five-foot deep by fifty-foot around pond. The water was filthy brown and murky and somehow managed to breed toads, tadpoles, and lots of earth worms. This was of course the perfect place for anxious and energy-filled kids to play and explore. My brothers and I built a makeshift raft out of old discarded construction materials. We had to learn how to make knots and tie-rods, and after a few failed attempts, we finally finished constructing our Tom Sawyer-like raft. An old white T-shirt served well for our sail and a half-broken tiki torch stick proved to be an efficient oar.

One late spring day in 1961, the weather was sunny, there was just the right amount of wind, and we knew it was the perfect day to launch. We drew straws to see which brave soul got to reign on the maiden voyage. I won.

When we got to the construction site, my two brothers tore off the old tarp in which we had covered the raft and we dragged it over to the water's edge. I was sure this was to be one of the best days of my life as I hopped aboard the "Kon-Tiki" as we called her, ready to set sail. I lifted the center pole and stretched out the T-shirt to catch the wind. My brothers pushed the raft into the water, and away I went. It was smooth sailing until I noticed that a few of the bent nails holding some flimsy plyboards together started to separate. My childhood ambition to become a Navy sailor quickly lost its appeal as the ropes unraveled and the pieces of wood drifted in five different directions. Down I went. I'll never forget my disappointment and failure, but worse than that, the sound of my two brothers laughing their heads off as I crawled out of the water covered in insects, seaweed, and mud.

It would be many years later while in the Boy Scouts that my friends and I would build a decent, seaworthy vessel, but I'm glad that someone else in my troop besides me drew the longest straw.

I'm not a big fan of fish. I know you're probably thinking, Wow, an Italian who doesn't like fish? That's like finding a Jewish person who doesn't like Matzo Ball Soup! Okay, I do enjoy fried calamari and marinated salmon once in a while, but if it is a choice between pasta and fish, I'll usually go for the lasagna.

Occasionally when I want to spice things up in the kitchen and I have some white fish available, this is my go-to recipe. It's quick and easy and takes under an hour to prepare.

Kitchen Tip: When grilling hamburgers, don't flatten them. This will make them lose both flavor and moistness.

Kitchen Tip: Make your life easier by using bottled vegetable or canola oil sprays to coat your pots and pans. Most of them are low in fat content and some are even flavored.

WHITE FISH FLORENTINE

1-1/2 pounds of white fish: perch, cod, orange roughy, halibut, or flounder

1/2 large red pepper, sliced

1/2 green pepper, sliced

2 medium roasted peppers

1/4 medium yellow onion cut into chunks

3 tablespoons red pepper jelly

1/4 cup milk

10 fresh basil leaves

2 bunches fresh spinach, rinsed cleaned and free of stems

Spray the bottom of a 10x18 glass baking dish with cooking spray. Lay the spinach leaves in the dish in a single layer. Cut the fish into small serving pieces and place them on top of the spinach.

Preheat the oven to 375 degrees.

Place all of the other ingredients into a blender and puree for one to two minutes. Pour over the fish and place in the oven uncovered for about forty minutes, checking for doneness after thirty minutes. The fish should be flaky, and the juices should run clear. Don't overbake.

Serve with a side salad, green beans, or rice pilaf. This will serve about four people.

Kitchen Tip: Don't add oil to your pasta water. It's a waste of money and doesn't allow the sauce to stick to the pasta. Also, never rinse the pasta under water. Drain your macaroni and cover right away with sauce.

I used to make house calls. No, I wasn't a doctor or a chiropractor; I was a TV repairman. I co-owned a very small TV and appliance store in a sleepy little shore town called Wanamassa (no doubt named after an Indian chief whose tribes long ago once occupied this eastern New Jersey shore). My business partner and I took turns making house calls. I preferred to work at the store and deal with walk-ins rather than subject myself to some of the most bizarre incidences with people you can ever imagine.

A Jewish friend of mine often used the phrase, "Oy Vey! I can tell you a million stories…". Well, I racked up a few doozies along the way and I want to share some of them.

One of the more "colorful" ones was the day I drove into the Sea Crest Apartment complex in a rather seedy section of Neptune City N.J.

I parked the van, grabbed my official RCA tube caddy, plus my condensed toolbox and walked up to the door of Apartment 102. I rang the buzzer and waited. After a courteous thirty seconds, I rang it again. I was just about to touch the buzzer again when the door opened and there stood a very large, hairy man dripping wet and wrapped in an unusually small towel. I introduced myself and made mention that it was exactly the time I was to arrive to repair his TV set. He just motioned for me to come in and mumbled something about losing all track of time. He ushered me into the living room and pointed to the TV and left.

After about five minutes, I had the set on and was just about to start diagnosing the problem when he appeared once again, drier than before, but still wearing the towel. I asked if he had a medium-sized mirror I could borrow, and he left again and returned with it. I set the mirror next to an ottoman and crawled behind the set. After removing the back cover, I started making some adjustments, first the horizontal hold, then the vertical hold, then the brightness and contrast. Before I could get to the next control, the man had stepped in front of the mirror and had dropped the towel. After getting an eyeful, I politely asked him to please re-locate himself so that I could see the front of the screen. With this, he edged himself closer to the TV and just stood there grinning. It's then that I realized that the customer had twisted and turned every single knob in the back of the set just to get some unsuspecting repairman to come undo his damage.

The more I ignored his "voyaging advances" the more seductive he became. I finally said, "It looks as if some child has been fiddling around with all the controls on the back of your set. It should only take me a minute or two more and you'll be back in business." After hearing this and realizing that I had no interest in anything other than getting paid, he left and came back with sweats and a T-shirt on. I wrote out the bill, charging him triple for my service and house call. He gladly wrote out a check and I left.

Another memorable service call was to a huge mansion along Ocean Avenue in Deal, New Jersey. These huge homes once belonged to presidents and members of congress long passed down to their present owners. The complaint: They couldn't change the channels.

As I pulled up to the circular driveway, I was instructed by the man-servant standing there outside the door. "We prefer that 'the help' use the side entrance." The bill suddenly went from $20 to $40.

To add insult to injury, I was asked to take off my shoes upon entering the foyer because they wouldn't want to get any grease on the alabaster white plush carpeting. Up the bill to $50.

I was escorted into the den, which was the size of an Olympic swimming pool and there in the corner was a 60-inch projection TV, the biggest one I had ever seen at that time. After the butler explained that they could only get one channel, I asked for the remote-control device. He handed it to me, and I started pressing buttons. The TV came to life, but it stayed on channel 2. I went over to the set and pushed a few buttons and the channels flew by immediately. I opened my trusty tube caddy and pulled out a nine-volt battery, installed it in the remote, and everything worked like a charm. No sooner had I written out the bill than the lady of the house entered to ask me if I had solved the issue. I said that the "issue" was a dead battery in the remote-control device, and she proceeded to tell me that it was only five years old and,

"Shouldn't they come with a lifetime warranty?"

I chuckled and said, "No madam," then finished scribbling out the bill and handed it to her. She glanced at the total, mumbled under her breath that the batteries shouldn't be her responsibility, and pulled out her checkbook from a drawer in the desk. She wrote out the check for $60 and I left.

This third call was a doozy and a half. The problem was that the TV in the living room wasn't working but the three others in the bedrooms were okay.

I arrived at the two-story house a few minutes early and was greeted at the door by a middle-aged woman and her giant Great Dane dog named "Sniffer." Odd name for a dog, I thought, but as long as he didn't jump on me and knock me over, I was okay with him.

First, I checked out one of the bedroom sets and it was fine. I went to the living room and there was no signal. "Can you tell me where your cable comes into the house, ma'am?" She explained that it was downstairs in the basement but seemed hesitant to let me go down there.

"It's a total mess down there. There's stuff all over and it's quite smelly."

"That's okay, I've seen worse," I said.

"Well, there's underwear drying on a clothesline down there too," she blurted out.

"I've seen that too," I said, trying to reassure her that I wouldn't dare invade her privacy. "Unless you have a kid locked up in a cage down there, I really don't care if I see your unmentionables."

As I started towards the basement door, she calmly said, "Not a kid." It took me a few seconds to realize what she meant, then she said that she would need to go and "ask permission." A few minutes later she emerged from the basement and said that it was okay. I marched downstairs with my toolbox in hand and sure enough, there in the corner was a man fully clad in leather and chains, locked in a huge metal dog cage. And yes, there were bits and pieces of undergarments strewn all over, and many, many chewed up dog toys and bones.

Apparently, Sniffer didn't know that the incoming cable wire wasn't one of them. Charge: $100.

Every so often I decide to just whip up something for dinner not even knowing what ingredients I have available. Such was the case of this next dish I call Creamy Tuscan Chicken Pasta. I invited three friends over for dinner and just let my creative kitchen skills flow. This one takes a bit of time, so when in a hurry, try something else. I was hesitant to put this one in my cookbook but after my guests raved about it, I decided to add it anyway.

CREAMY TUSCAN CHICKEN PASTA

2-3 medium-to-large chicken breasts
3 tablespoons paprika
1/8 cup olive oil
3-4 pats of butter
1 medium sweet yellow onion, chopped
5-6 medium garlic cloves, minced
2 small cans of low-sodium chicken broth
1 cup half-and-half
6 oz. cream cheese, softened
4-6 oz. chopped or diced sun-dried tomatoes, in oil
6 oz. baby spinach leaves (no stems)
1 tablespoon Italian seasoning
1 teaspoon dried basil leaves
12 oz. penne pasta (pre-cook for 7-8 minutes only)
Salt and pepper
1 package Knorr Parma Rosa Sauce Mix (a substitute for this is in the recipe)
Grated parmesan cheese
Optional: cherry tomatoes

Rinse the chicken breasts in cold water and place them on a cutting board. Do not pat dry. Season them first with salt and pepper and then paprika on both sides.

Heat up a deep, Teflon-coated Dutch oven or sauce pot for about five minutes on medium to high heat.

Add the olive oil once the pot is heated and add the pats of butter. Braise the chicken breasts for three to four minutes on each side, making sure they do not burn. Turn them over a few times and pre-cook them until they are crispy on the outside and pink on the inside. Set them aside.

De-glaze the pot with a wooden spoon and add the chopped garlic and onion. Cook for about five minutes or until the onions are tender, stirring occasionally.

Add the chicken broth, half-and-half, Italian seasonings, and the dried basil then heat to boiling. Lower the temp and drop the chicken breasts back into the pot. Cover and let cook on medium heat for about five minutes. Uncover and remove the chicken breasts to a cutting board. Dice the chicken into small, bite-sized pieces, making sure they are completely cooked. Place the chicken in a bowl and cover with aluminum foil. Keep warm in a 200-degree oven until later. Raise the heat again on the pot and let the mixture come to a boil.

Prepare the Parma Rosa sauce mix using only about a half-cup of milk. Stir until smooth and add to the boiling mix. (If you don't have this sauce mix you can substitute by using a couple tablespoons of tomato paste, a quarter cup of corn starch, a small amount of olive oil, a half-teaspoon of garlic powder, a dash of paprika, a teaspoon of dried parsley, a pinch of sugar, and a half-cup of whole milk). Mix thoroughly and stir into the broth mix to thicken it.

Once the broth mix is thickened, add the cream cheese and the sun-dried tomatoes then stir until the cheese has melted. Add the pasta into the pot and add more whole milk if needed to make it creamy but not dry. Heat the pasta with the broth mixture for about five minutes on medium heat. Finally, add the spinach leaves and cook just until they are wilted. Place the pasta in a large serving bowl, add the diced chicken to the top, sprinkle grated parmesan cheese on top, and surround the bowl with cherry tomatoes, if desired. Lastly, sprinkle some parsley leaves on top and serve immediately. This recipe will serve about six people depending on the size of the chicken breasts used.

If you were to ask any member of my family what my nickname was growing up, they would have all said, "the professor." Unlike my two younger brothers, *my* chosen sport was science. I always had my head in a book and I never stopped wondering "WHY."

When I was nine years old, I remember reading in our school newspaper that Ford Motor Company was planning to build a nuclear-powered automobile. It was to be called the "Nucleon" and the experimental design was to be powered by uranium. I wanted so much to be the first "kid" to ride in that atomic car. As luck would have it, it never went into production, which is probably a good thing. No scientist could predict exactly *what* would have happened if someone smashed it in the rear.

In the late 1950s and early 1960s, everything was atomic this and nuclear that. Russia launched Sputnik. People were worried about atom bombs being dropped. Schools practiced air raid drills. Toy manufacturers made a killing by selling space-related rocket ships, atomic ray blaster guns, walking and talking robots, and lots more. But there was one item introduced in 1967 that interested me more: the microwave oven. The first ones built were huge– about five feet tall and weighed around 750 pounds. In addition, they cost around $5,000. We didn't get our first one until 1976. Now I can't imagine cooking even breakfast without one, so, to celebrate the wonder of the microwave oven, here is a recipe that makes using it more fun.

BAKED POTATO SOUP

6 slices of bacon
2/3 cup flour
1 cup yellow onion, chopped
6 cups or 3 small cans of low-sodium chicken broth
4 cups diced baked potatoes (equivalent to 6 medium potatoes)
2 cups whole milk
1/4 cup fresh chopped parsley
2 teaspoons garlic powder
2 teaspoons dried basil leaves
2 teaspoons salt
1/2 teaspoon black pepper
1 cup grated cheddar cheese
1 cup sour cream

Wash and hand dry the potatoes. Place them on a microwavable plate and microwave them on medium-low for about fifteen minutes. Pierce the potato with a fork and it should easily glide in about two inches or so if done. Once they are cooked, let them cool and then cut them into small, bite-sized pieces including the skins. Cut the bacon into small pieces and place the bacon and onion in a deep Dutch oven. Heat on medium heat until the bacon grease melts and browns the onion and bacon bits. Use a whisk and stir the flour into the bacon mixture, cooking for about two minutes while stirring constantly. Gradually add the chicken broth while increasing the heat to high and continue whisking to prevent lumps from forming. The mixture will begin to thicken. Add the potatoes, milk, sour cream and the other spices. When it begins to boil, lower the heat and add the cheddar cheese. You can add chopped or sliced green onion before serving. Oh, and remember, the microwave will come in handy to heat up a bowl of leftover soup in just minutes. This recipe serves 8 to 10 people.

Here's another tip: In a pinch you can use a slotted spatula to separate the egg yolk from the white. If it's Teflon coated, the yolk will just slide off and the white will simply drip through the slots.

This next recipe is for a delicious dessert that you will almost always find at an Italian dinner party. It makes a great light dessert when serving a heavy pasta or thick, hearty vegetable soup. And it's easy to make, coming in at under one hour.

ITALIAN PEAR CAKE

1-1/2 cups all-purpose flour
1/3 cup cornstarch
1/4 teaspoon baking soda
1-1/2 teaspoons baking powder
3/4 cup sugar
3 eggs, at room temperature
1 small container of mascarpone cheese
2-1/2 tablespoons canola oil
1/8 teaspoon salt
2-3 very ripe and un-bruised pears (yellow Anjou work best)
Lemon juice

Preheat the oven to 350 degrees.

Lightly grease and flour a 9-inch round 2-inch deep cake pan

Clean and peel the pears, removing all dark blemishes and skins. Remove the cores and chop one-and-a-half pears into small, bite-sized pieces. Slice the remaining pears into thin, one-eighth-inch slices. Douse lightly with lemon juice to prevent them from turning brown. Place the eggs and sugar into a medium bowl and beat until light and foamy. Add the mascarpone cheese and continue beating until smooth. In a separate bowl, mix together the flour, baking soda, baking powder, salt, and corn starch. Mix the dry ingredients thoroughly and then add the oil. Stir to combine. Fold in the cube-sized pear pieces and pour into the prepared cake pan. Layer the sliced pears on top of the filling in a rosette pattern. Sprinkle the top pear slices with sugar. You can also sprinkle sliced almond pieces on top before baking. Bake for approximately forty-five minutes, checking with a toothpick for doneness, and continue baking if the center is not completely firm. The cake can be served warm or cold with a side of vanilla ice cream or fresh whipped cream. This serves about eight people.

A warm and sunny day in Pisa, Italy

While traveling through many parts of Italy, I noticed that many restaurants serve "Tuscan" foods. Tuscany has gotten a lot of attention in the past decade or so, and much of that influence has drifted its way into the restaurants of America. Almost every mainstream Italian eatery has some sort of dish from Tuscany. Poor Milan (the city of designer clothing and expensive cars) gets hardly any recognition for some of their most favorite foods, one of which is this rice dish that originated in the Lombardy region of Italy in the city of Milan in the sixteenth century. This recipe makes a great side that can be served with just about any fish or meat main dish. I should caution you though: it contains a spice called Saffron which is fairly pricy but go ahead a splurge here. It's worth it.

RISOTTO ALLA MILANESE

1 box of Arborio Italian Rice or Jasmine Rice (approximately 14 oz.)

1 large can (32 oz.) low-sodium chicken broth

1/4 cup dry white wine

1 stick unsalted butter

1/2 cup grated parmigiana cheese

1 small onion, finely chopped

1/2 teaspoon Saffron spice

Black pepper to taste

Melt the butter in a large, cast iron pan. If you don't have cast iron, use a deep Teflon-coated fry pan. Add the onion and sauté for about five minutes using medium heat until the onion is soft and slightly browned. Add the rice and cook for five or six minutes stirring constantly until the rice is slightly crispy. Add the wine and lower the heat. Cook until the wine evaporates. Slowly add the chicken broth (reserving 1/8 cup for later) into the pan and continue cooking on low heat for about fifteen minutes. Mix the saffron spice into the reserved chicken broth and set aside. When the rice is nice and creamy, remove from the heat. If it looks too dry, you can add a little more wine to make it moist. Add the saffron mix just before serving. Sprinkle a little black pepper and parsley on top as well as some grated cheese and serve warm. This makes about four good-sized servings.

Freshman year (1962) for me was one of my biggest fears. We were the first students to attend a newly constructed high school and it was huge. I was used to going to smaller, more intimate schools where the student body was around 100 kids. Raritan Township High had an enrollment of about 800. I, like all the other newbies, had to learn a whole new and radical class schedule. I was used to just sitting in one classroom for seven hours and now I had to attend eight classes; some in different rooms, all in one day. One saving grace for me was signing up for both wood shop and industrial arts.

In 1958, Congress passed the National Defense Education Act, and federal money was allotted to high schools to encourage young teens to pursue technological skills. This was mainly as a response to the Russians sending up the first orbiting satellite called Sputnik. The program got off to a very slow start and some faculty members found a sneaky way of getting the kids involved. I, like most of my peers back then, was hooked on oldies music. Japan took notice of this and began importing small, hand-held transistor radios which ran on batteries and took the teen market by storm. Everyone wanted one.

Our science and shop teachers started a contest among the students. The student who created the most unusual wood or metal object would vie for the big prize: a new 6-transistor Koyo brand portable radio.

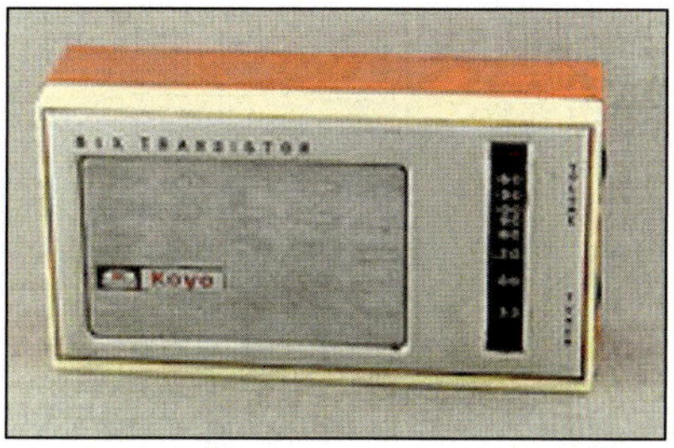

Some of my woodshop classmates built wooden ash trays, salad bowls, or bookshelves, and one enterprising young man built a tiny little wooden suitcase to fit a stack of very popular 45 RPM records. I was determined to win that radio. I started thinking about something I could build that no one would ever think of. After pondering this and that, I hit upon an idea. I would use both my skills in wood shop and metal shop to build my very own croquet game. For those of you who don't know what croquet is—well, it's a lawn game where there are up to six players. There are six wooden balls about the size of a large baseball, six wooden mallets and eight three-sided metal rungs. These are placed about eight feet apart on a grassy area and your colored ball is hit with the mallet and needs to travel through each of the metal tunnels. This game resembles golf, except the balls don't go into holes in the ground.

Using the wood lathe, I made the poles and heads for the mallets, and with the band saw, cut out squares of wood for the balls. I used the vertical sander to round out the balls then stained them and painted each with two different colored stripes. I did the same with the mallets to color coordinate the colors with the balls. In metal shop, I formed and bent the rungs and painted them white along with a nice rack to hold all the pieces. It took me about half the school year, but when it was all finished, I was so proud. The deadline date came and each one of the finalists stood next to his project, explaining to the judges how it was made. One by one, they gazed at the six remaining contestants, and slowly all were eliminated except for me and Johnny Santini. He made a wooden doll house. It was really nice and very colorful, with fake plastic windows and a realistic chimney. The judges gathered around my croquet set and whispered to themselves while staring at both our projects. Then they stepped over to the doll house. One of the judges placed his hand on the roof of the house and, well, let's just say that the integrity of the structure just wasn't there. The roof collapsed and fell into the bedroom and living room, leaving the fake occupants in a pile of rubble. My facial expression at that moment could only resemble the one on the Mona Lisa. My grin was a cross between wicked and regret. I tried not to laugh just as the judges awarded me 1st prize.

When we were kids, many Sundays always consisted of at least three things we could count on: church, Sunday gravy, and a "ride in the country." The "country" for us was just getting out of the house and traveling at least five miles from home. On occasion we would be speeding along some rural road and whoever was driving would suddenly slam on the brakes, causing the car to come to an abrupt halt and leaving a dust trail behind, then we would all shout out "BLUEBERRIES!" All four car doors would swing open and we kids would grab our ball caps, buckets, and pails and head out into the bushes. Finding wild blueberries in New Jersey wasn't all that difficult, but you had to be careful you didn't wander on to anyone's property. After an hour or so, with our vessels brimming with fresh blueberries, we would head on.

There is one sure way to store them. Don't wash them, but after picking off the stems, put them in freezer plastic bags, push out as much air as possible, and pop them into the freezer. They will stay for months.

Here is my recipe for my favorite breakfast or anytime muffins. These always get rave reviews from my friends and family.

BLUEBERRY CRUMB MUFFINS

Muffins:

1-3/4 cups all-purpose flour

2-1/2 teaspoons baking powder

1 cup sugar

1/4 teaspoon salt

2 large eggs, at room temperature

1/2 cup canola or vegetable oil

3/4 cups whole milk

1-1/2 teaspoon vanilla extract

1-2 cups frozen blueberries (depending on size)

Flour for dusting

Crumb Topping:

1 1/4 cups all-purpose flour

3 1/2 tablespoons soft light brown sugar

3 tablespoons granulated sugar

1 1/4 teaspoons baking powder

1/8 teaspoon salt

3/4 stick, or 8 tablespoons, unsalted butter, melted and cooled

Preheat oven to 375 degrees. Pre-grease twelve large metal muffin tins with shortening, or you can use medium cupcake liners (about 15 to 18).

Combine all the ingredients for the crumb topping and use a fork to break up large chunks into small, pea-sized pieces. The mix should be moist but not runny. Add a little more flour if necessary, then set aside. Place the frozen blueberries in a mixing bowl and keep in the freezer until ready to use.

In a medium bowl, add the eggs, sugar, and oil. Beat with a mixer on low speed for about one minute. Add the milk and vanilla and mix for a few more seconds.

In a large bowl, add the dry ingredients for the muffins and mix well. Add in the egg mixture and beat with a mixer for two minutes.

Remove the blueberries from the freezer and sprinkle some flour on them. (This step will prevent the blueberries from sinking to the bottom of the muffin while baking.) Coat them well with the flour and then drop them into the prepared batter. Don't overmix. Divide the batter into the muffin tins, filling about 3/4 full and then evenly divide the crumb topping on each one.

Bake for thirty minutes (check with a toothpick for doneness at about twenty-five minutes). The toothpick should come out clean. Remove from oven and let them cool ten minutes or more before removing them to a cooling rack. The recipe makes about eighteen regular-sized muffins or twelve larger muffins.

They say a young man never forgets his first car "incident." I certainly didn't. I had learned to drive the family station wagon so I could have some independence and take the younger kids to school and batting practice. I never signed up for mother transport day, although it was assumed that I had. We had a 1966 Chevrolet Chevelle wagon big enough to hold six kids and at least a dozen pieces of camping gear for a family outing. We went camping a lot.

I remember my mom asking if I would take her grocery shopping. Mom never learned how to drive, and she was deathly afraid to get behind the wheel and learn. She made neither a good front seat nor back-seat driver. I had her claw marks in the seat cushions and dashboard to prove it. Some of her favorite "yells" were: "Why are you going so fast?" and, "Why are you driving so close behind that other car?" or, "Why didn't you turn when I pointed?" You can see how those sorts of distractions could annoy a driver. One day we were on our way back from the Shop-Rite Supermarket with at least ten full bags of groceries in the back of the wagon. The seats were folded down to make room for the bags on the flat surface. As I'm coming up to a light, mom screamed "THAT GUY IS GONNA RUN THAT LIGHT!" I slammed on the brakes and just as we got out of the intersection, the bags of groceries started flying forward. Next thing I knew, there were cans of vegetables in my lap, apples and oranges under my feet, and the dashboard was covered with everything you needed to make a good stew. One of the oranges got stuck under the brake pedal and as I went to push further to stop, my legs were spritzed with orange juice. Finally, we came to rest on the side of the road, and although dazed and confused, we were all right. After a few minutes of calming down my mother, I went back to assess the damage. If it weren't for the ten-pound bag of flour that had burst, it would have been an easy cleanup. After that day, I just gave mom money for a cab.

While vacationing in Naples, Italy a while back, I took a small excursion boat out to the Isle of Capri. Once on the island, I took the Funicular (cable car) up to the top of the mountain to the center city. From this vantage point, you could almost see the coastline of mainland Italy. It was one of the most beautiful spots I have ever been to. It was mid-afternoon and I sat down at a local outdoor café. A waiter came along carrying a tray of small, chilled flutes filled with limoncello. He offered me a complimentary taste. I was immediately smitten with this incredible drink. I ordered a regular glass and I was in heaven. I will say, it is quite potent and a sip or two (especially while sitting in the sun) will make you a bit loopy. But you must try it. I decided to make some home-made Limoncello, and although it took a month, it was certainly worth it. Here is my recipe with a couple of variations:

LIMONCELLO

5 organic (preferably Meyer Type) lemons
1-1/2 cups 150-proof Everclear grain alcohol
3 cups of water
1 1/4 cups sugar
1-quart mason jar with seal and lid
Cheesecloth

Thoroughly wash and dry the lemons to remove any wax from the outside. Peel off the lemon skins making sure you don't include any of the white "pith" in the peel. Place all the skins in the quart jar and add the everclear. Place the jar in a brown paper bag and put it in a cool dark place to sit for at least two weeks. Once a week, shake the jar.

After two weeks, prepare the syrup. Place the sugar and water in a saucepan and bring to a slow boil. Once the sugar is dissolved, remove from heat and cool.

Place a piece of cheesecloth or a fine mesh strainer over another quart jar and pour the lemon/alcohol mixture through the strainer and into the jar. Add the syrup and stir. Transfer this to a nice decorative bottle and place into the freezer to chill. Serve cold in a chilled glass.

This will make a quart of Limoncello

Variations:

Add a whole vanilla bean to the peels before storing for a delightfully different taste.

Add the juice from all the lemons strained through cheesecloth into the jar with the peels and then decrease the amount of water in the sugar/ water mixture to compensate. You may need to increase the amount of sugar as the juice will make the final product a bit more tart.

Use 50 to 75-proof vodka instead of Everclear but let the peels ferment about a month instead of two weeks.

Double the recipe and make a few more bottles to give as gifts. A nice printed label and yellow ribbon on the top will make a great Christmas gift.

If you can find imported Sorrento lemons to use instead of Meyer's, the taste will be more authentic to what they make in Naples.

When my grandfather, Pasquale Carfora, died, the local newspaper, *The Jersey Journal,* did a feature story on his life. Gramps was the last surviving peanut vendor in Jersey City.

I didn't have a close bond with him because he didn't speak any English and was hardly ever around. When he did retire from his job as a mason, he couldn't stand being idle. He decided to fashion an old buggy into a peanut wagon. It was stocked with one-gallon glass jars filled with every kind of candy and nuts that kids would want. He sold bubblegum, Mary Janes, Sugar Daddy's, Bits-O-Honey, root beer barrels, candy cigarettes, and Turkish Taffy. In addition to regular roasted peanuts, he sold walnuts, pistachios, and my favorite sugar-coated crunchy peanuts. Candy was a penny apiece and nuts were either 5 or 10 cents a bag. In the summertime, he also hawked cold watermelon slices and popcorn. Pops made lots of money by wheeling his wagon down Freeman Avenue into Lincoln Park. There he would wait for all the kids to get out of school, and the school just happened to be right across from the park, through which most of the kids took shortcuts to get home. A lot of the kids were from poor families but always had a few pennies or a nickel to spend on candy from Pops. Every day, Pops would bring home an apron filled with coins and give them to Gram. She would count the money, then stash it away in jars. She would also put a few coins in a small purple handkerchief, tie the ends together, then put it into her apron to give out to her favorite grandkids. I can remember it like it was yesterday, running into the house and Grandma's face would light up like a kerosene lantern when she saw us. "Hugs for Grandma!" she would say, and we never missed an opportunity to hug her. Right after, she would reach into her apron and pull out that purple handkerchief, open it, and hand us a nickel or dime. She would press the money into our little hands, fold our fingers tightly, and say in the sweetest voice, "Daah! Here … This is for you … Don't tell the other kids. You're special." For years, I thought I was the only special kid in Grandma's life.

I remember when my grandmother's old Kelvinator refrigerator broke down after owning it for about twenty-five years. Gramps took out his old gunny sack and filled it with all the jars of coins from Grandma's pantry. Dad dragged the money bag into the old Studebaker and drove them to downtown Jersey City to Sears to purchase a new one. They wheeled the bag of money into the showroom and Gramps picked out a nice new Sears icebox. The clerks were not at all thrilled that they had to sit down and count out $325 worth of assorted coins.

My nephew, Nate Serio, and I enjoying dinner at the World Trade Center in New York City, July 2018

If you are searching around for something to do with all those plump, tart and fragrant Meyer Lemons you still have left over from the Limoncello recipe, here's a treat you can't pass up. It goes great as a dessert after a heavy meal, but don't forget to add some lemon sorbet with it before serving:

LEMON LOVERS SCRUMPTIOUS LEMON LOAF

Cake:

1/2 cup canola oil

1-1/2 cups all purpose flour

3 large eggs

1/4 teaspoon salt

2 teaspoons baking powder

1 cup sour cream or low fat plain yogurt

2-3 tablespoons of lemon zest

2 tablespoons of lemon extract
(not flavoring or juice)

1 cup sugar

Preheat the oven to 350 degrees. Grease and flour a 9"x5" loaf pan.

In a large bowl with a hand mixer, add the eggs, sour cream and sugar and mix on low speed until combined. Add the oil slowly while mixing slowly. Add the lemon extract and zest and combine. Add the flour, baking powder and salt, and mix with a wooden spoon until combined. There might be some lumps, but they will not interfere with the baking. Pour into prepared pan and bake on the middle rack of the oven for approximately 45 minutes. Test the center with a toothpick. It should come out clean. If not, continue to bake and check every 5 minutes until it is solid in the center. Remove from oven and let cool completely before removing from the pan.

Glaze:

1 cup confectioners sugar

3-4 tablespoons of freshly squeezed lemon juice

Combine and stir until you reach a nice thick pouring consistency. Add more sugar or juice until desired thickness is achieved. Pour over the cooled cake and let dry before slicing. Your can freeze the loaf wrapped tightly in saran wrap for up to 6 months.

LEMON RICOTTA CHEESECAKE

Crust:

2 cups graham crackers or vanilla wafers (pulsed into crumbs)

1/3 cup sugar

1/4 tsp salt

7 tablespoons un-salted butter (melted)

Cheesecake:

3 8-oz packages of regular (not lite) cream cheese, room temp.

1 cup whole milk ricotta cheese, room temp.

1-1/4 cups sugar

2 tsp pure vanilla extract

3 large eggs and 2 egg yolks, room temp.

2 tablespoons all purpose flour

3/4 cup freshly squeezed lemon juice

2-3 teaspoons fresh lemon zest, no pith

Lemon Whipped Cream:

1 1/2 cups heavy whipping cream

1/2 - 3/4 cups confectioners sugar

2 teaspoons lemon extract

2 teaspoons knox unflavored gelatin

5 tablespoons warm water

2 teaspoons lemon zest

In a food processor, pulse the crackers and add the sugar and salt until you get fine crumbs. Add the melted butter and stir well to combine. Grease liberally a 9” spring-form pan on the bottom and sides with Crisco. Preheat the oven to 325 degrees.

In a large bowl or food processor bowl, beat the cream cheese and ricotta until smooth. Add the sugar and vanilla. Add the eggs and yolks and continue beating until smooth. Stir in the flour and combine until smooth. Add the lemon juice and zest and combine with a spoon. Don’t over-beat.

Wrap the spring-form pan in heavy duty aluminum foil so that it comes up about 2-3 inches on the sides. Try using one sheet to avoid seams.

Place the spring-form pan into a deep roasting pan and pour the cheesecake batter into the pan. Fill the outer pan with enough HOT water to come up about 2-3 inches. Try not to splash the water into the cheesecake batter.

Bake in the preheated oven for about 1 hour. Check for very light browning at the top. It may require another 15-20 minutes to bake. At the point where the top is just slightly browned, turn off the oven and let the cake continue baking undisturbed for about 45 minutes. The center might still be a bit wiggly.

Remove the cheesecake from the oven and let cool on stove top. Once it has cooled, you can remove the side—but first run a plastic knife around the perimeter to loosen it, if it isn’t already. Lay a piece of plastic wrap loosely over the cake.

Refrigerate the cheesecake for about 4 hours before adding the whipped topping.

In a medium but deep bowl, pour the whipping cream. Place the mixer blades in the cream and place in the freezer for a while. In a small cup, add the water and then sprinkle the gelatin on top. Let it set for a few minutes to soften. Stir it a little, then place in microwave for 5 seconds until it becomes syrupy. Let it cool completely.

Remove the cream from the freezer and add the confectioner's sugar, vanilla, lemon extract and lemon zest. Whip on high for a few minutes until you get soft peaks. Slowly pour in the gelatin while beating on high for a few minutes until stiff peaks form. Frost the cooled cheesecake and decorate with lemon slices, or you can pipe additional whipped cream dollops around the outer edge before serving. You can slice and freeze pieces of cheesecake between pieces of waxed paper for later, but I would freeze them without the whipped topping. The whipped cream and cheesecake can stay out of the fridge for about 4 hours without wilting.

Cuffing! This is a word that few people living outside the east coast of the U.S. would know, including those who are not of Italian heritage; so, let me explain. If you take your right hand and make a scoop out of it, then swiftly bring your hand up to the back of someone's head and swipe just the top part with a forward force, then you are cuffing someone.

When we were kids, we got cuffed a lot. Dad would do most of the cuffing, but sometimes when one of us kids got cuffed, we passed it along to whomever was standing by at the time. I'm not sure where this originated, but it looked a lot like something The Three Stooges did, and my dad just loved The Three Stooges.

One time while having dinner, I said something of which my father disapproved. My dad quickly cuffed my sister Rene and then told her to pass it on to me. I ducked under the table. It's always good to know when a cuff is coming your way so you can be evasive. Sure, I got away with it that time, but someone always managed to sneak in a good cuff when I wasn't looking. "That was for that last snide remark," they would say. An impending cuff doesn't have an expiration date.

Kitchen Tip: Spray a cheese grater inside and out lightly with a baking spray before grating. Cleanup will be much easier.

The bulldozers woke me up early with their thunderous movement down East Road. As I peered out the window, my first thought was that someone new was moving into the neighborhood. While still rubbing the sleep from my eyes, I continued to watch as this giant flatbed truck pulled up. WOW! It was the biggest "Caterpillar" I had ever seen. My curiosity was piqued now as I rushed out of bed, threw on some clothes and purposely skipped a few of my morning do's. I'll have to gobble down my breakfast, I thought, if I wanted to get to the construction site before getting on the school bus.

East Road was usually a very quiet neighborhood. Nothing much ever happened there. There were no schools, no factories, no large department stores; in fact, it was so quiet that the government decided to put up a top security Nike base not far from where we lived. I guess they thought that no one would ever suspect there was an army munitions base secretly hidden behind the old Scheckley farm. I remember reading the signs that said "GOVERNMENT PROPERTY—KEEP OUT UNDER PUNISHMENT BY LAW."

That sign was serious enough for my friends and me. We never even tried to go over the fence once.

I managed to get myself spruced up enough to pass mom's morning inspection and went down to breakfast. My two brothers were almost finished with their Cheerios and were about to rush out of the house when I mentioned the construction crew. I don't think they were as excited as I was that morning, but I knew that would change soon.

I could still feel the coldness of that damp April morning as we walked down the sidewalk toward the bus stop. There were about four or five burly looking men standing around the flatbed truck wearing their orange and brown overalls with bright yellow hard hats. It looked as if they couldn't figure out how to get the Caterpillar off the truck, but I think they were just taking a coffee break. As I got closer, I felt a shiver run over me. I thought of that massive machine just sitting there with its giant claws tucked in. It sat idle, anxiously waiting for one of the men to set it free to devour the earth, down the trees and perhaps anything else that might get in its way. Two of the men yelled out a good morning to us as we walked past. We answered them with a quick hello. One of them chucked a smoldering cigarette butt my way, coughed and then walked away. They seemed pleasant enough, but they gave me the feeling that we had better keep our distance.

Mrs. Burdick was out in her yard tending to her bees just as she did every morning. She was just coming out of one of the giant metal cages as I neared her. "How's it going?" I asked. "We're doing just fine, young man," she answered, and went back to her task. She was a nice old lady and always gave out the best stuff on Halloween.

"There it is!" I shouted, pointing to the vacant lot adjacent to Mrs. Burdick's, house. There, sitting on the corner of East Road and High View Circle was a sign that said in big bold lettering, "ON THIS SITE … 3 LUXURIOUS SPLIT-LEVEL HOMES FROM THE MID 20'S."

For the next month, we would watch that construction crew every morning and evening as we came and went from school. My brothers and I would make bets on how much progress they would make by the end of a day. I thought it was something special to watch a pile of raw materials just sitting there, soon to end up being somebody's actual house. As it turned out, however, it wasn't until December that the foundations were finally laid and the main construction began.

I could remember going down into the basements of the unfinished houses to ice skate. The basements would fill up with rain water and freeze. The bad part was that there were all these pipes and fixtures sticking up out of the ice and you had to be a pretty good skater to avoid hitting them. It was extra special on the days when it was snowing real hard. Having the day off from school, I would wander over there and climb into the basement. I loved sitting there in that open framed house. There I was, all bundled up with five pairs of socks on, a bulky down parka, heavy gloves, a scarf and my dad's old aviator helmet. I could sit there for hours watching the snow fall, feeling secure in that basement lair. When there was no auto traffic going down East Road and it was very quiet, I could almost hear the snowflakes as they landed on the open rafters of that framework. The house would have an incredible echo within, so that even the slightest sounds would become amplified.

I really enjoyed the times I spent there with my thoughts and just by myself.

I guess the construction company ran out of operating money because those three houses stayed in that unfinished condition for the next three seasons.

There was also a pond on East Road. It was high above the homes on a hill near the old Scheckley farm. It was a pretty good-sized pond that was brimming full of tadpoles, crayfish and probably a hundred other slimy creatures we didn't even know the names of. I remember the day my brothers and I built a raft out of old logs and scrap wood. We spent a good part of the day looking for just the right pieces and getting enough heavy rope to tie them all together. We worked hard at it, and by sundown it was ready for launching. I was the official guinea pig. We launched her near the shallow end, and it was steady going until the raft got caught on a pole sticking up in the pond. It was there that the rope broke, the logs split apart and I wound up in the murky waters surrounded by animals and gush. I managed to crawl back to shore to save myself. I was covered from head to toe with mud, and my clothes were unwashable. Once we got back to the house, my brother ran upstairs to get me some clean clothes. They both took turns pouring buckets of water on me in the back yard, and when I was clean enough I stripped out of the wet things and into dry clothes. I was almost presentable when I heard my sister call out that it was supper time. I quickly got out a shovel from the shed and dug a small hole. I buried by shirt, shorts, socks and underwear. As it turned out, I couldn't fool anyone. My mother noticed the little mud balls in my ears and then came by for a closer inspection. Once she got a good whiff of me she flew into a rage and ordered me into the bathroom. I was not to come out until spring, or until my father got home, whichever came first. I wasn't scared of my dad. He knew that my first spill in the local pond was to be celebrated and I knew he would understand.

I had many friends on East Road. There was the set of twins who lived down past the butcher shop in the dell. They had a great big front yard with lots of trees and a tree house in one of them. I often went there to play because they had a lot of the neatest things. Their dad was always building them scooters or swings or something new.

I always liked it when mom sent me to the butcher shop for meat. If we got a big order, Mr. Savoros would give us a free popsicle. The twins were always jealous of us because their mother never bought meat. They were vegetarians, so they never got free ice cream.

Almost every neighborhood has at least one odd occupant. On East Road we also had one. We had an actual witch who lived in the big mansion up on High View Circle. We never knew her name; we just knew she was mean and rotten. If you accidentally wandered onto her property, she would bark at you like a rabid dog and chase you away. She had a huge black cauldron on her lawn, and rumor had it that she boiled little kids in it if she caught them there after dark. My friend Tommy told me that his brother spied on her spreading honey on the bark of her dogwood tree, so that she could catch insects to eat for dinner. She certainly was strange and most of the neighborhood kids knew to stay far away from her and her gloomy old house.

Dad came home from work one day and told everyone that we were going to have to move from East Road. I didn't like hearing that. This happened to us all too many times growing up. As our family grew, we were always needing a bigger house.

"I have friends here," I said. "I love my school, I love the pond, I love the twins and Mrs. Burdick," I went on. "I love the old Scheckley farm and the butcher shop. I even love that old witch who lives up on the hill. I don't want to leave here, Dad!"

Dad looked at me sadly and I could tell he wasn't convinced of my sincerity. "We need a bigger house," he replied. "We have another kid on the way, and we need another bathroom, a bigger kitchen, and … well, we just need to move." I became very sullen, dropped my head down and started to walk away.

Dad put his hands on my shoulders and turned me around, looked me right in the eyes and said, "That's why I bought that new house they just finished building down at the end of the street."

This next recipe is one that almost every grandmother has made at one time or another. Mine was no exception. It's a classic for sure, but with a different twist.

GRANNY'S BANANA BREAD

1 1/2 cups granulated sugar

1 cup Crisco shortening

3 eggs

4 tablespoons mayonnaise

2 teaspoons of baking soda (dissolved in 1/8th cup of warm water)

3-4 overly ripe bananas (mashed up and mixed with 3 cups of flour)

Cream the sugar and shortening. Mix in the eggs and mayonnaise. Add the baking soda mixture and then the banana-flour mixture. Stir until just mixed. Don't over mix. Pour into a greased and floured loaf pan (approximately 8"x10"x2" deep. Bake at 350 degrees for 45 minutes, then check the center with a toothpick. If the toothpick is still wet, cover with foil and bake for additional time until done. Dust with powdered sugar before serving.

Kitchen Tip: Here's a tip on how to get the most or least amount of flavor from your garlic bulb. To obtain a mild garlic flavor, slice the garlic a bit thicker and saute in olive oil until tiny bubbles form on the outer edges. Remove the garlic to prevent it from becoming bitter. For a stronger flavor, mince the garlic and saute on medium heat until the pieces are a deeper brown. Immediately add your other ingredients and incorporate the garlic and oil into the food.

When I was going to school at Monmouth College in Long Branch, New Jersey, there was a shortage of dorm rooms for those who were not taking a full curriculum. I managed to secure a room in the Newman Center, a medium sized place that housed the campus priest and out-of-town visitors who needed a place to stay while touring the college. I befriended Father Dan Kellaher and we became good friends. Not only did we jog together, but I taught him a few lessons about cooking. Since he was a full-blooded Irishman, he enjoyed learning all about the art of Italian cooking.

One Sunday evening, after tasting my Cappellini with pesto sauce, he immediately drove over to the local nursery and brought himself a dozen fresh basil plants so that he could grow his own and make this wonderful pesto sauce. I think he made that a yearly ritual from then on. This recipe will make enough pesto for a pound of pasta.

LEN'S PESTO

1/3 cup of good quality virgin olive oil

2 cups of freshly picked basil leaves, minus the stems (packed)

1/2 cup of grated cheese (I prefer a Locatelli/Pecorino mix)

3 tablespoons of unsalted butter (softened)

1/4 cup of pinoli (pine) nuts

2-3 medium cloves of garlic

1 teaspoon salt

Using a food processor is the best way to make this sauce. If you don't have one, make sure the garlic and pine nuts are minced really fine and the basil leaves are cut into really small pieces.

If you are using a processor, add all the ingredients at once and pulse until smooth. If you plan to freeze the pesto sauce, omit the cheese and butter and add it once the sauce is defrosted. You can also vary the recipe by combining a handful of walnuts and a couple tablespoons of pine nuts. This can be used on any type of pasta, but make sure you cook the pasta al dente and don't rinse it. Toss the hot pasta with the pesto and add additional grated cheese before serving. You can use plastic ice cube trays to freeze the pesto (minus the cheese and butter), and once frozen place them in a well-sealed plastic bag. They will stay good for over a year.

Here is another of my quick 1/2-hour prep dinners. When served with some garlic bread and a glass of chilled red wine, you'll have a mini feast in the middle of the week:

LINGUINI AGLIO OLIO (PASTA WITH GARLIC & OIL)

1/3 cup of extra virgin olive oil
5-6 medium cloves of garlic (finely minced)
1/4 teaspoon crushed red pepper
1/3 cup chopped fresh parsley
1 pound of linguini or thin spaghetti

Heat the olive oil in a fry pan on low heat for a few minutes. Drop in the minced garlic and saute it just until lightly browned. The secret is not to burn the garlic. Once slightly browned, remove the pan from the heat and let it sit for about 5 minutes. Cook the pasta until it is *al dente* and drain it, reserving about a cup of the boiled water. Add the pasta directly into the fry pan and heat it for a few minutes. Add some of the pasta water if it seems too dry. Add the red pepper flakes and the parsley, then serve with grated   or parmigiana cheese on top.

Growing up in a family of 11 was murder. Christmas wasn't exactly overflowing with boughs of holly. I was a middle kid and the oldest of the boys. My parents never had very much money, and although love was abundant, gifts were scarce. I remember one such Christmas when I was about seven years old. We kids were not even sure we were going to have a Christmas tree that year. It was one of the coldest winters on record for New Jersey. Wood and coal were the highest priorities, and most of the money was spent keeping the furnace supplied with fuel. As the season grew near, we were told that we were only getting one gift apiece and that we were to appreciate any hand-me-downs that we got. My grandmother always managed to brighten things up for us a little. When she visited, she would sneak a few nickels into our hands. It wasn't much, but it did put smiles on our little faces.

Dad worked two jobs most of his life and never really had much time to spend with us kids. He did manage to see to it that we always had a warm house and food on the table.

As Christmas day got closer, I was wondering how I could stretch a dollar and ten cents to buy all the gifts I needed to get that year. I realized that mom's and dad's gifts would cost that much alone. One Friday evening after school, dad came home and we had a family meeting. He told us that he had some friends down at the local B.P.O.E., which was known as the Elks club. A bunch of the guys were going to get together and throw our family a Christmas party. They were also going to invite two other poor kids who lived down the street from us.

Well, we were all so excited we couldn't sleep that night. Mom got us up early the next morning and we dressed in our warmest sweaters and gloves. It had snowed again the previous night and the air was as crisp as apple pie. I can remember waiting on the front porch of our house for the van to come by and pick us up. As we waited, we took turns making frosty clouds from our breaths. We didn't have to wait too long. Around

8:30 a Volkswagen bus pulled up and a tiny little pudgy guy got out. He opened the side door and we all piled in. Jeffery and Kenneth from down the street were already in the van and they were just as excited as we were. Mr. Ben told us all to sit down and he would explain what they had planned for us that day. You could hear a pin drop.

"First of all," he said, "we're going to have to do a little shopping for Christmas presents for our families." We all looked at each other in surprise and wondered where we were going to get money to do that, when all of a sudden he reached down into his jacket pocket and pulled out a stack of brand new shiny silver dollars. One by one he handed each of us five of them. I looked down at the coins and thought how heavy they were. I had never had a dollar coin before this.

"Now," he said, "That takes care of the money part," and off to the department store we drove. When we arrived at the Family Circle store, we were greeted by the store manager, who informed us that they had opened up the store early just for us and that we had a little more than an hour to buy our gifts. There were also about five or six of the nicest clerks who worked there who came in extra early just to help us shop. We each had a clerk to ourselves and they took us up and down the aisles of the store. They pointed out things that were on sale and kept a running total of how much we had to spend. With their help, that $5 really went a long, long way. After we paid for our treasures, they took us into the back of the store where they wrapped our gifts in special Christmas wrap with bright bows and cards attached. No sooner was that done when Mr. Ben thanked all the helpers and the store manager, then whisked us away in the van, speeding to our next surprise stop.

We drove for about half an hour. We were so busy yapping and giggling about our gifts and things, the time just flew by. We arrived at the Elks' Lodge in Red Bank, and the bus stopped outside the entrance on West Front Street. As we got out, Mr. Ben escorted us into a brightly lit room all decorated with streamers, balloons and red- and green-covered tables with little lighted Christmas trees on them. Over in the corner was a giant eight-foot spruce tree all decorated with garland, ornaments, lights, and even candy canes. The room smelled of freshly baked cookies and fragrant pine tree scent—two of my favorite smells. As I looked around the room, I noticed the stage set up with a gingerbread house on it. Just then a couple of young ladies dressed in elf suits came in and announced the beginning of the Christmas party. We all sat down, and they brought us cups of hot chocolate with marshmallow fluff on top and a tray of freshly baked cookies. Each of us was given a mesh bag filled with apples, oranges and Christmas candy to take home. There were Christmas tunes playing in the background, and the ladies went around and got all of us up to dance on the dance floor while they sang along to the musical selections.

Finally Santa arrived and handed each and every one of us a gift with a special tag made out in our own names—and it wasn't even Christmas Eve yet. We tore into the packages with wild anticipation.

After a while the elves quieted us all down and we were treated to a puppet show. They put on the Christmas Story play and it was the best I could ever remember.

When we got home late that afternoon and told mom and dad about our day, I can remember mom saying that it's this special time of year when people should get together and help make wonderful, lasting memories for those who are less fortunate than others. I'll never forget that day for the kindness of strangers who helped make the day one of my fondest Christmas memories ever.

If you have ever been invited to a party thrown by an Italian family, you knew it would not only be a wild party, but you would not leave until you've met at least 30 cousins, eaten at least a half dozen ethnic foods, and probably danced with one big hairy uncle you thought was a woman because you sampled too much of the home-made Chianti. Italians know how to party, and they will celebrate just about anything to have one. When you are baptized, you get a party. When you become an eagle scout, they throw you a party. And God forbid, if you had to marry your 17-year-old girlfriend because she was "with child", there would be a party. Of course, they would rename it a graduation just to avert any dubious gossip.

Italians don't skimp on the food, either. One call to Vito at the local butcher shop and you know the feast he will prepare will rival those incredible banquets that were served at state dinners back during the ancient Roman conquests. There would be prime rib, lasagna, stuffed mushrooms, three or four antipasti dishes, soup, fried calamari, manicotti, trays and trays of fresh deli cold cuts, clams on a half shell, chicken piccata, tortellini salad, spaghettini carbonara, veal Marsala and maybe even a roast beef or two. You can also count on at least a dozen different desserts such as cannoli, tiramisu, assorted Italian pastries and, of course, trays and trays of colorful and flavorful cookies. Aside from the traditional wedding cookie made with a sweetened almond dough, baked and dusted with powdered sugar, there is another favorite of mine—the pignoli cookie. These cookies are rather expensive to make but they are so worth the time and trouble. I try to make them around the holidays when I am entertaining, and they are always a big hit at MY parties.

PIGNOLI COOKIES

8 oz box of almond paste (do not use tube paste)
1/4 cup granulated sugar
1/2 cup confectioner's sugar
3 tablespoons all-purpose flour
1 large egg white
8 oz pignoli nuts (also called pine nuts)

Preheat the oven to 300 degrees. In a food processor, break up the almond paste into small chunks. Add both sugars and the flour. Pulse until you get a fine crumb-like mixture. Add the egg white and pulse until a dough forms.

Prepare a light metal baking pan with parchment paper. Wet your fingers and pull off a quarter sized piece of dough. Roll the dough to form a ball. Place the dough ball down onto a plate of the pignoli nuts while pressing slightly. The cookies should be still rounded but with a flat bottom. Place the cookies about an inch apart. Place in the preheated oven for 15 minutes using the lower third of the oven. After 15 minutes, rotate the pan and bake another 10 minutes until you get a very slight brown color. Don't overbake the cookies, or the pine nuts will become bitter tasting and they will no longer be soft and chewy. Cool them on the tray for about 15 minutes and transfer to a cooling rack. Dust with confectioner's sugar before serving. If you prefer a more intense almond flavor, you can also add a 1/4 teaspoon of almond extract to the dough while pulsing. The cooled cookies can be frozen in a plastic bag for about 2 months. This recipe makes about a dozen-and-a-half cookies, more or less.

The cookie jar was a very big part of the Italian kitchen. I could always remember getting new cookie jars when one would get accidentally dropped or if the lid would go missing from another one. I have a vivid memory of a large, red strawberry cookie jar with a green leaf lid sitting on top of the refrigerator in my grandmother's house. It was placed so high that, even if you could manage to pull up the baby's high-chair next to the fridge and climb up, you couldn't get to it. Once we moved to our own house, we got another one as a housewarming gift. This one was a big brown ceramic model of a friar monk dressed in a big brown robe with a rope around its waist. At the bottom were the words, "Thou Shalt Not Steal". Even when the grownups didn't offer us cookies, we kids just thought we were borrowing them, not stealing them.

We acquired another cookie jar when the good monk was pushed off the back of the counter by Mitzie, our overly playful 10-year-old Calico cat. This one was a large reddish-and-white painted Guernsey cow. It only took about three weeks to get severely mutilated by my younger brother, and she lost her left hind leg. We had to prop her up with a box of rosebud wooden matchsticks. No matter what shape the cookie jar was in, you could always count on some really delicious cookies to be found inside. Sometimes it was those second rate no-brand vanilla or chocolate sandwich cookies that cost a dollar a pound; or, if we were lucky, neighbors and relatives would visit and periodically replenish our supply of homemade ones.

Since I love to bake, there are always some of my favorite cookies hanging around our house. I tend to give a lot away, but I always manage to freeze a bunch so if that late-night coffee craving hits, I have a few sweet treats to go with it. The following recipe is one of my favorites, as well as a lot of our friends'. I always make them around the holidays and for dinner parties, and they are always a big hit. They are nice and soft, chewy, and they smell amazing; and they are super easy to make and store.

LEN'S CONFETTI COOKIES

- 1/2 cup of unsalted butter (1 stick at room temperature)
- 8 ounces of regular cream cheese (room temperature)
- 1 egg
- 1/2 teaspoon of almond extract
- 1/2 teaspoon of orange extract or 1 tablespoon of orange juice concentrate
- 1 box of white cake mix (store brand is fine)
- 1/2 to 1 cup of colored rainbow sprinkles
- 1/2 to 1 cup of confectioner's sugar

In a medium bowl, cream the butter and cream cheese. Add the egg and mix well. Add the extracts and the cake mix. Use a wooden spoon to combine and then add half of the colored sprinkles, mixing well.

Cover the dough with plastic wrap and refrigerate for at least an hour or two. The colder the dough, the less sticky it will be to handle.

Preheat the oven to 350 degrees. Using about a tablespoon of dough, roll into a ball and then roll the ball in the powdered sugar. Roll the ball completely in the colored sprinkles and place on a greased baking pan about 2 inches apart. Bake for approximately 10 minutes or until very lightly browned and a bit soft in the middle. Try not to overbake them. Cool in the baking pan for 5 minutes and then transfer them to a paper towel to cool completely. You can store them in one of your fancy cookie jars—perhaps a cow that has all of its legs attached—or you can put them in a Ziplock bag and freeze them for up to 3 months. This recipe makes about 40 cookies. Don't forget to share!

My dad loved to make his "goombas" happy. If you don't know what a goomba is you might want to ask an Italian. Here is my take on it. Goombah (sometimes goomba) is a slang term regional to the New York area used to describe an Italian-American. It can be mildly derogatory, but not on the same level as dago, guinea or wop. When dad had his restaurant, he would often make special dishes to serve to his favorite goombas. These people were his favorites. They would often bring their families into the pizzeria late, order a few bottles of guinea red wine (cheap stuff), and sit for a couple of hours enjoying my dad's cooking. He would whip up some fried calamari as an appetizer, dish out some homemade escarole soup, and for an entree, lasagna or baked ziti with his special black olive bread.

Olive bread is not something you will see on the menu of most Italian restaurants because it is a lot of work to make and you really must like black olives. It is sort of like focaccia—thick and chewy and bursting with pizza-like flavor. I'm including it in my cookbook because you should not go through life without trying it at least once. The following recipe will make 2 large loaves, enough for at least 6 goombas.

BLACK OLIVE BREAD

2 large pizza dough rounds (frozen is ok)
4 cans of black olives (sliced)
2 medium sized sweet vadalia onions
3-4 cloves of garlic
1/4 cup of white wine (chardonnay is good)
olive oil
fresh parsley
salt and pepper
Italian seasoning

Chop the onions into medium sized chunks and set aside in a bowl. Slice the garlic cloves very thin and set aside. Drain the olives of their water and chop them into small rice sized pieces.

Coat a large frying pan with olive oil and saute the garlic on medium heat for about 3 minutes. Add the onion and cook until the onion is soft. Add the olives and a handful of freshly chopped parsley. Add the wine. Add a pinch of pepper and a pinch of salt. You can eliminate the salt if you wish.

Stir and cook the mixture for about 15 minutes on low heat.

Cut the thawed dough rounds in half, and with a rolling pin roll out and stretch the dough to form a rectangle about 6"x12". The dough should be about 1/2" thick. Use a heavy duty aluminum baking tray. Grease the bottom and place one piece of dough on the bottom. Spread half of your olive mixture over the dough and place the second piece over this one. Seal the edges with a fork to seal in the juices. Brush the top of the dough with olive oil and sprinkle with Italian seasoning. Complete the second loaf just like this one. Bake the loaves in a preheated 350 degree oven until golden brown. Serve warm.

So, you probably have noticed that there aren't too many recipes in this cookbook for vegetables. And you probably also notice that not too many people who write cookbooks would include a recipe for a vegetable that doesn't seem to get much attention these days: Brussels sprouts. I must admit, I wasn't too fond of them either; but a while back I was dining out with friends at a local bistro and I asked the waitress about this oddity on the menu for Brussels sprouts. She told me how the chef prepares them, and the minute she mentioned garlic and bacon I was intrigued. Before I could either turn my nose up at them or gladly opt for them as a side veggie, she offered to bring me a taste.

I was amazed at both the smell and the flavor of them and I decided to try and re-create them at home. After getting a few more trade secrets from the waitress, she spilled the beans with the chef's technique. "The magic is in the bacon," she said. "Use hickory flavored style bacon and you can't go wrong."

After a few failures and a Teflon pan that I will NEVER get clean again, I came up with what I think is an amazing favorable recipe for the lowly, bitter tasting and poorly neglected Brussels Sprout. Try it and see if you agree with me.

GARLIC & BACON BRUSSELS SPROUTS

10 slices of premium Hickory Smoked bacon
6 medium cloves of garlic (minced)
3/4 cup low sodium chicken broth
1/4 teaspoon ground black pepper
2-3 pats of butter
3-4 teaspoons of virgin olive oil
Pinch of oregano
Pinch or two of salt
2 pounds of fresh Brussels sprouts

Clean and wash the Brussels sprouts in cool water. Drain. With a sharp paring knife, cut an "X" into the stem of each piece.

In a large deep skillet, place the slices of bacon and cook them over medium heat until the edges are slightly crisp. Turn the strips half way through the cooking time. Place the bacon slices on paper towels to drain. Once cooled, use your hand and crumble the strips of bacon into small pieces.

Pour out most of the bacon grease from the fry pan into a cup and save it in the fridge for use with other recipes.

Heat 2 pats of butter and the olive oil in the pan and add the minced garlic. Cook the garlic until the edges start to get lightly browned. Don't overcook—three or four minutes is all you will need. Add the Brussels sprouts to the pan and pour in the chicken broth. Add the salt, pepper and oregano. Cover and cook on medium heat for approximately fifteen minutes. Poke a fork into the thickest of them and it should slide right through. If they are not tender yet, continue cooking for additional time. Drain the chicken broth from the pan, add the left over butter, the bacon crumbles, and if you want even more flavor add a bit more of the bacon grease. Heat for a couple of minutes. Stir and serve right away.

On my 18th birthday, my mother sat me down in the kitchen and poured us each a small glass of Chianti. "Today, you are a man," she said. And so in keeping with an age-old tradition in the Italian culture, she handed me a small gold foil box. I opened the box and took out the small square of white protective fiber. Underneath lied a strange looking gold horn. "What's this?" I asked. I wasn't ready for the story she began to tell, but I listened intently. "This is called a Corno," she said, rolling the RRRRR's like a good dialect teacher. "When a boy becomes a man, he is presented with a Corno by either his nonna or his mother." She went on. "It is not something you can buy for yourself. It must be given." At this point, my curiosity got the best of me and I asked her what it meant. "It is meant to protect you against the evil eye, the devil, and even Satan," she explained. "It will keep you safe." My first thought was why she hadn't given it to me a year earlier when I really needed it. I had a terrible accident on my bike and ended up in Saint James hospital for two weeks with broken bones and a concussion. I didn't press the issue, and she continued. "Some people call it a Cornicello, which means a small horn in Italian. The amulet was adapted from both Greek and Roman mythologies dating back to the 5th century B.C., and it's said to promote fertility, virility and good luck." I picked up the tiny, twisted golden horn and held it up to the light. "Where did you get it, Mom?" I asked. "Well, it came from a small souvenir shop down in Little Italy, and I didn't pay full price for it either," she said. Once again, I was curious and asked her what she meant by that. Did she bargain with the sales clerk, or did she have a discount coupon? "Oh, no," she explained. "According to tradition, one cannot pay full price for a Corno, and it must not be bought for yourself or the wearer will have nothing but bad luck." I sipped on the Chianti and listened to the explanation. "It was 20 bucks, but I asked the salesman to give me back a penny. He obviously knew what I meant and handed me back a shiny 1967 penny."

About a week later, I went into Prager's Jewelers and bought myself a beautiful 18-carat gold rope chain and put my Corno on it. Soon after, I noticed that I was beginning to get darker facial hair, and the mustache that I had ever since I was age 7 had finally started to show. I remembered mom mentioning the word virility. Hmm, I thought. Was this really a magical link from adolescence to manhood, or was it just my normal hormones kicking in? I didn't question it, but I am very superstitious about my horn and it has never come off since … well, except for that one time when I needed to have an MRI done on my shoulder.

Kitchen Tip: If you are sugar conscious, you can use sweetened apple sauce as a substitute for any granulated sugar in a recipe. If the recipe is too watery, add a tablespoon of flour to thicken it up before proceeding.

Here is another vegetable recipe that you won't find in a lot of cookbooks. I adapted this recipe from one I found in an old newspaper, the Asbury Park Press in N.J. The original recipe used walnuts, but I found them to be bitter tasting when mixed with the lemon juice. This recipe is a great one to take along on a summer picnic or better yet as a side dish for that holiday gathering you were planning. Makes about 6 servings.

LEMON PESTO ZUCCHINI

8-10 thin Zucchini about 12" long (grated skins and all)
1 small sweet yellow onion (minced)
5 medium cloves of garlic
3-4 tablespoons extra virgin olive oil
1/4 cup of hazelnuts
1/4 cup of grated parmigiana cheese
10-12 medium basil leaves (no stems)
2 small to medium lemons

Place the grated zucchini and onions in a small microwave bowl and cover with plastic wrap. Microwave on high for about 3 minutes until they become soft.

Place the hazelnuts in a small fry pan and toast them over medium heat for a few minutes while stirring them constantly. They should become very fragrant once toasted. Coarsely chop the nuts.

Using a zester tool, remove the yellow zest from the lemons. Cut and juice the lemons, removing the pith and pits. Reserve the juice.

In a food processor, blend the nuts, lemon juice, zest, basil, garlic, olive oil and a pinch of salt and pepper. Pulse until smooth.

Combine the sauteed vegetables with the pesto mixture and heat in a pan on low heat until just warm. Sprinkle with grated cheese before serving.

SIMPLE APPLE COBBLER

1 package of refrigerated sugar cookie dough (1 pound 16oz. or more)

3-4 medium sized apples (honey crisp, fuji, or gala types)

2-3 tablespoons fresh squeezed lemon juice

1 teaspoon cinnamon

1/8 teaspoon ground nutmeg

pinch of ground cloves

1/2 cup granulated sugar

1/4 cup light brown sugar

1/2 cup flour

5-6 pats unsalted butter

Peel and core the apples and slice them into 1/4 inch slices. You will need approximately 2-1/2 cups.

Preheat the oven to 350 degrees.

Remove the cookie dough from its wrapper and press it into a 9"x12" glass baking dish. Cover the bottom completely.

In a small bowl, mix the two sugars together.

In another small bowl, mix the apples with lemon juice and 2-3 tablespoons of the mixed sugars. Add the spices and mix again until combined.

Add the flour to the remaining sugars and mix until combined. Add the pats of butter and combine with a fork until you get fine crumbs. Sprinkle the crumbs over top of the apple mixture. Bake for about 35 minutes or until the top starts bubbling.

Cool slightly before serving. Top with whipped cream, or better yet, vanilla bean ice cream.

One of my earliest memories of music was when my dad found a huge old console radio-phonograph just sitting on the curb waiting for the trash man. With the help of his buddy, Ken, they dragged it onto the back of his '49 Ford pickup and lugged it home. It sat in the corner of the living room for at least two weeks before we even plugged it in. I was just knee high to the top lid and could barely reach it standing on my tippy-toes.

One afternoon, I came in from school to the sound of an old 78 RPM record playing on the console. The sound was both tinny and scratchy, but all in all a catchy tune by Guy Lombardo and his Royal Canadians called the Tennessee Waltz. As I inched closer to the speakers the sound got worse, but being the curious little tot that I was, it didn't stop me from pulling up a dining room chair to the big old wooden monolith to have a look. I got up on the chair, stood in front of the giant cabinet, and lifted the heavy wooden lid. There was a big flat black record spinning around and around so fast that I could hardly make out the big word DECCA on the label in the center. I examined the tone arm—without touching, of course—and watched intently as it moved from the outer edge to the inner one at a pretty fast pace. Once the music stopped, the arm magically picked itself up and moved back to the beginning and it started playing all over again. I was in my glory watching this mechanical marvel belting out the Tennessee Waltz all over again and again.

Eventually, mom came in and saw me teetering on the edge of the chair and abruptly snatched me off and set me back down on the floor. "You can watch and listen from there, young man," she said. She selected another large black record and placed it on the rotating platter and pushed a lever. She closed the top lid and then replaced the chair back at the dining room table. I waited until she was safely out of sight in the kitchen and quietly dragged the chair back to my viewing position. The music started again. This time, the label was a bright yellow with the letters MGM and a nice picture of a lion. It was a lot more interesting than the DECCA label, but this time the music was awful. The tune was saying something about Mr. Froggie going a-courtin' by somebody named Burl Ives. As much as I loved watching this mechanical wonder, the sound of Mr. Ives just hurt my ears. If I were brave enough, I would have just changed the record myself, but then mom would certainly know I was disobeying her and there would go my allowance. That Christmas, I received my very own Mickey Mouse record player, but it was a bit disappointing. It didn't play those large, fast, flat, black records like mom and dad's—only little yellow Peter Pan ones; and they played just about every song I had already heard from watching the Mickey Mouse Club on TV.

As I mentioned previously, most of the recipes in this book are pretty quick and easy. I left this one for last because it is a bit more challenging, but it is so worth the time and effort if you have the time. Rainy or snowy days are great for cooking up a pot of this wonderful dish called Minestrone Soup. The good thing about this recipe is you can use just about anything you have sitting around in the fridge. There are a few rules, but you can get as creative as you want and it will still turn out great. Also, this is a meatless dish; so you can indulge any vegans in your family. Let's get started.

ITALIAN MINESTRONE SOUP

This recipe will make about six full bowls of soup but you can double the recipe if you have more guests, or want to put some up in jars for later.

Optional veggies: parsnips, turnips, savoy cabbage, small new white or red potatoes, leeks, fresh spinach or Swiss chard.

It's a good idea to prepare all of your vegetables ahead of time.

I like using the largest stock pot I have, so if you do decide to add more ingredients while you are preparing this soup you will have plenty of room in the larger pot.

1/4 cup of extra virgin olive oil

1 small to medium onion (chopped into small chunks)

3 medium sized carrots (leave skin on and cut into slices)

3 celery stalks (preferably with leaves) washed and cut into slices

3-4 cloves of garlic (minced)

3-4 green and/or yellow squash (leave skin on and dice them—see recipe)

1 1/2 cups of frozen green beans (about 1" pieces)

1 large can of diced, crushed, or stewed tomatoes

3 small cans of low sodium chicken broth

1 teaspoon of crushed rosemary or 1 sprig of fresh rosemary

1 teaspoon of dried thyme

2-3 tablespoons of fresh chopped parsley

1-2 teaspoons dried basil

1 bay leaf

1 can of red kidney beans

1 can of white beans (great northern, or cannellini)

1 teaspoon paprika

Grated Parmesan cheese (sprinkle on before serving)

2 cups of cooked ditalini or elbow pasta (cooked al dente)

Heat the olive oil over medium-high heat for about 3 minutes. Add the onions, carrots and celery. Stir the veggies and cook for about 7 minutes. Add the minced garlic and cook an additional 3 minutes. For the squash, cut off the ends and then slice them lengthwise into 3 pieces. Hold the slices together and cut them across into small chunks about 3/4 inches thick. Add the squash, green beans and any other cut-up vegetables you want to add. For parsnips, do the same as the carrots, but cut the wider pieces into smaller chunks. Cut the small round potatoes into 4 pieces before adding to soup. For the spinach, tear the leaves in half and discard any stems.

Add the tomatoes, the seasonings, basil, parsley, paprika, rosemary, bay leaf and thyme. Add a tablespoon of salt and a teaspoon of ground pepper. Add the cans of broth.

Bring the soup to a boil, and then turn the heat down and let simmer slightly covered for about a half hour. Add the cans of beans, including the juices. If the soup seems too thick, or if you prefer more broth, add more cans of low sodium chicken broth until you get the consistency you desire. Remember, the more vegetables you add, the more broth you will want to add. Cook for another half hour on medium to low heat. Remove the bay leaf.

If you are going to serve the soup now, cook the pasta and add it to the individual bowls as you serve. Top with grated cheese.

If you are going to put the soup in jars, don't add the pasta. Bring the soup to a rolling boil and fill the hot clean mason jars, leaving about a half inch below the rim. Place the canning lid on top and slightly tighten the ring. Cool on a counter, then fully tighten the lid the rest of the way. I like storing the jarred soup in the fridge, but they will also stay on a shelf for about 3-4 months. Check the seals before storing and make sure they sealed properly. If the jar didn't seal, remove the cap and lid. Place a folded piece of wax paper over the opening and secure with a rubber band. Place the jar in the microwave and heat for a few minutes until you see some bubbles coming up through the soup. Carefully remove from the microwave and take off the wax paper. Clean the top edge with a wet paper towel and immediately place the sealing lid back on and tighten the cap. Let sit and make sure the seal seats. You can also freeze the soup in Tupperware, but let it cook completely before freezing; and again, don't add the pasta until serving.

Kitchen Tip: Add a dollop of room temperature sour cream to your scrambled eggs after removing them from the fry pan. They will stay softer longer, and be a bit creamier in texture.

Well, my family and friends, we have come to the end of this book. I hope you have enjoyed reading it as much as I have enjoyed putting it all together. I have also enjoyed sharing some of my childhood memories with you. I hope I made you laugh a little, sigh a little, and perhaps share a little of my life with you, your kids, and your grandkids. Thanks to all of you who were kind enough to send in your stories and recipes.

Buon Appetito!
Lenny Ricci

Enjoying a laugh and a Belgian Waffle in Ghent, Belgium with my friend Anna

Food Index